ESOL BOOKS

Read and Write every day

Upper ESOL Literacy Workbook

Dave Butler

Information for teachers

Acknowledgements

Many thanks to several people who have made this book possible. Firstly, thank you to Linda McFall and Kyle Bettley for breathing life into the initial publication from ESOL Books, which has now also led to this series. In addition, thanks to Susan Leitch, the author's partner teacher for many years, especially for her enthusiasm to discuss materials and teaching techniques, often long after the end of class! Thank you to my partner Christine Rosser for her constructive feedback. Thanks to everyone at Glasgow Clyde College for their support, without which this book couldn't have happened. Many thanks also to my dad, Alan Butler, for his expert proofreading. Thank you to Anh Viet Tran and Kim Hoang Nguyen for their expertise to ensure accurate information in the text about Vietnam in Unit 3. The images used in this series are from www.depositphotos.com, www.istockphoto.com, www.pixabay.com and www.unsplash.com.

About the author

Dave Butler has been teaching groups of basic ESOL Literacy learners for almost 20 years. He holds the CELTA, DELTA and SQA TESOL Literacies qualifications. He's also a teacher trainer on the CELTA and SQA TESOL Literacies courses at Glasgow Clyde College. He enjoys learning Spanish, playing Subbuteo and banter with his family and friends.

Disclaimer

With the exception of myself, the texts focusing on individuals in this book have been invented for educational purposes. The names and details in these texts are the products of the author's imagination. Any resemblance to actual persons, living or dead, or actual events is purely coincidental.

Rationale behind this series

One of my aims while teaching basic ESOL literacy groups is to support them on their path to the next level. I have noticed over the years that when students make this sizeable jump they then struggle as coursebooks for beginner classes include longer, more complex texts and tasks, not to mention instructions and, of course, more advanced vocabulary and grammar. I have often thought that this sudden step up must be overwhelming for many students. Indeed, I have known many move back to the class from which they were promoted. The idea of this book is to provide a bridge between the two levels.

How to use this book

This Workbook accompanies the course book, Read and Write every day Upper ESOL Literacy Student's Book, which is intended as a resource for teachers to use in class with groups of learners. The tasks in this Workbook consolidate the work done in class. As homework is crucial to the progress of ESOL students, I hope that this book provides learners with valuable extra practice.

More materials, classroom ideas, audio and videos

As just stated, a Student's Book is available now. In addition, a Teacher's Book is planned. The Student's Book includes tasks for classroom use, helping learners continue to progress with their literacy and numeracy while also supporting them with more advanced areas such as grammar. For an Answer Key to this book, extra materials including Power Point slides, links to Kahoot games, audio and videos for students as well as teaching tips and ideas for teachers, go to our website: www.esolbooks.com, navigate to 'Read and Write every day Upper' and then click on 'Extra Resources.' The website also offers you the chance to sign up for our mailing list to be kept up-to-date with our latest news.

Other books available

Read and Write every day
ESOL Literacy Student's Book / Workbook / Teacher's Book

A series aimed at groups of basic ESOL Literacy learners (pre-entry), including stimulating tasks to improve your students' reading, writing, phonics and basic numeracy. The Student's Book includes graded texts and personalised writing tasks for learners to do in class. In addition, the Workbook includes controlled practice for homework and the Teacher's Book contains advice on how to stage the material, plus a bank of games and flash cards.

Writing for SQA National 5
Student's Book and Teacher's Book

This series is for teachers preparing groups of students for the ESOL National 5 exam writing paper (upper intermediate level). The Student's Book includes model answers for the 4 writing tasks (formal and informal e-mail, report, essay), incorporating analysis of the key language used in each task type and practice for the learners throughout. The Teacher's Book provides guidance on staging the material as well as a comprehensive Answer key.

Thanks and feedback

Many thanks for buying this book. I hope that your students find it useful! Please send any feedback to the author: davebutler@esolbooks.com.

Dave Butler
ESOL Books

Contents

Unit		Page
1	Nice to meet you!	5
2	Free time	29
3	How's the weather?	53
4	It's a beautiful world	69
5	What's the matter?	85
6	What are you wearing?	105
7	Technology	125
8	It's broken!	145
9	What's your job?	159
10	We had a great time!	171
11	The summer	185

Unit 1

Nice to meet you

Nice to meet you!

Fill in the gaps.

~~your~~ with live Who from What
English name get free like do Where are

What's (1) __your__ name?

Hi, my (2) ____________ is Fatima.

(3) ___________ are you from?
Where (4) _______ you live?

I'm (5) _________ Sudan but
I (6) ________ in Scotland.

(7) _______ do you live with?

I live (8) _________ my friend Suad.

(9) _________ do you do in
your (10) _________ time?

I (11) ________ football and You Tube.

Why (12) _______ you learning
(13) _______________?

I want to (14) _______ a job.

Mohammad

A. Reading

Read about Mohammad and answer questions 1-7 below.

My name is Mohammad and I'm 28 years old. I'm from Sudan but I've been in the UK for 2 years. I live in Glasgow now with my friend Omar. I really like Glasgow. I like my college and the people but it rains a lot. I go to college four days a week. I like my teachers and the students in my class and I like learning English. I like watching You Tube videos and playing football with my friends.

1. What's his name? Mohammad.
2. How old is he? ____________________
3. Where is he from? ____________________
4. Who does he live with? ____________________
5. Why does he like Glasgow? ____________________

    ____
6. Why does he like his college? ____________________

    ____
7. What does he do in his free time? ____________________

    ____

B. **Writing**

Copy and write about Mohammad.

My name is Mohammad and I'm
28 years old. I'm from Sudan
but I've been in the UK for 2
years. I live in Glasgow now with
my friend Omar. I really like
Glasgow. I like my college and
the people but it rains a lot. I go
to college four days a week. I like
my teachers and I like learning
English. I like watching YouTube
videos and playing football with
my friends.

C. **Vocabulary**

Fill in the gaps.

with people ~~is~~ students years

friends college learning videos been

My name (1) __is__ Mohammad and I'm 28 (2) ____________ old. I'm from Sudan but I've (3) ___________ in the UK for 2 years. I live in Glasgow now (4) _________ my friend Omar. I really like Glasgow. I like my college and the (5) ____________ but it rains a lot. I go to (6) ________________ four days a week. I like my teachers and the (7) ________________ in my class and I like (8) ________________ English. I like watching You Tube (9) _____________ and playing football with my (10) _____________.

D. **Spelling**

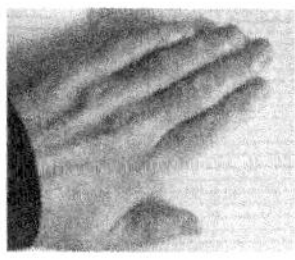

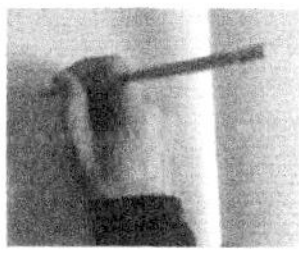

Cover the text above and fill in the gaps.

My na__e is Mohammad a__d I'm 28 yea__s ol__. I'm fr__m Su__an b__t I'__e bee__ in the UK for 2 year__. I li__e in Gla__gow n__w wi__h my frie__d Omar. I real__y li__e Gl__sgow. I l__ke my col__ege a__d t__e peo__le bu__ it ra__ns a lo__. I go to c__lle__e fo__r d__ys a w__ek. I __ike my tea__hers an__ t__e stud__nts in my cl__ss a__d I li__e lear__ing Engli__h. I li__e wat__hi__g You Tube vi__eos a__d pl__ying foot__all wi__h my fr__en__s.

E. **Writing**

Copy the sentences but add capital letters and full stops.

1. my name is mohammad

   My name is Mohammad.

2. i'm from sudan but i live in glasgow

   ____

3. i've been in the uk for 2 years

   ____

4. i live in glasgow with my friend omar

   ____

5. i really like glasgow

   ____

6. i speak arabic and english

   ____

7. i like learning english

   ____

8. i'm a student now

   ____

9. i go to college from monday to thursday

   ____

10. i like watching you tube videos in my free time

   ____

I'm a student

A. Vocabulary

Find the words from the text about Mohammad and circle them. Some words go down!

~~name~~ ~~from~~ live been years

student like love want

o	l	i	v	e	c	f	c	w	f
o	i	i	w	s	y	n	h	y	r
p	k	n	a	m	e	b	t	l	o
k	e	c	n	o	a	d	t	i	m
i	r	a	t	n	r	n	t	n	n
m	b	e	e	n	s	l	o	v	e
g	c	i	j	e	s	a	n	y	y
w	s	t	u	d	e	n	t	g	m

B. Writing

1. Fill in the gaps to write sentences about yourself.

My name is ____________________. I'm from ____________________ but I live in ______________________. I've been in ____________________ for __________________. I like ____.

2. What's your name? Where are you from? What do you do in your free time? Write about yourself.

____

____

____

____

3. Cover the text and write it again.

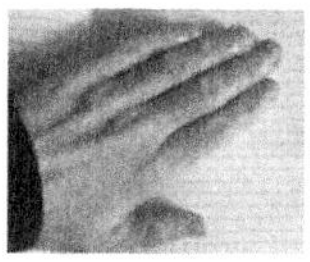

____

____

____

____

I like cooking and swimming

Grammar: and / but / or

Circle the correct word.

1. I like cooking **or / but / and** swimming. I cook every day and I go swimming at the weekend.
2. I like football **or / but / and** I don't like tennis.
3. I like You Tube **or / but / and** Tik Tok. I watch videos on these two apps every day.
4. Do you want to go to the gym **or / but / and** go swimming tomorrow? I don't have time to do both, just one of them.
5. Ali is a very good student. He goes to college **or / but / and** he does his homework every day.
6. There were 10 **or / but / and** 11 students in class yesterday.
7. What day is it? Is it the 10th of January **or / but / and** the 11th?
8. We can drink water in class **or / but / and** we can't eat food.
9. - Would you like tea **or / but / and** coffee?
   - I would like coffee please.
10. I have coffee with milk **or / but / and** sugar. I like a little milk and two spoons of sugar.
11. What would you like for dinner? Would you like rice **or / but / and** pasta? Which one?
12. I like juice **or / but / and** I don't like milk.

Numbers

A. Numbers: 0 - 100

Copy and fill in the gaps.

0 1 3 4 5 7 8 9 10

12 13 15 16 18 19

21 22 23 25 26 28

29 31 32 34 35 36

37 39 40 42 43

45 47 48 50 51 52

54 56 57 58 60

62 63 64 65 67 68

69 71 72 73 75 76

78 79 81 83 84

86 87 89 90 92

94 95 97 98 100

B. Reading

Read the words and write the number.

a. ten	10	e. one	____	i. forty-eight	____
b. five	5	f. thirteen	____	j. sixty-one	____
c. twelve	____	g. twenty	____	k. eighty-four	____
d. eight	____	h. seventeen	____	l. fifty-two	____

C. Spelling

Fill in the gaps

10	__en	22	__w__nt__-t__o	91	__i__e__y-__n__
11	__lev__n	24	t__en__y-f__u__	93	n__n__ty-t__ree
12	t__el__e	31	__hir__y-__n__	100	o__e h__nd__ed
13	__hir__e__n	33	t__i__t__-__hr__e	200	tw__ hu__dr__d
14	__o__r__e__n	44	f__r__y-f__ur	300	th__e__ h__nd__e__
15	fi__t__en	48	__or__y-__ig__t	400	f__ur h__n__r__d
16	__i__t__e__	56	f__ft__-s__x	500	__i__e __u__d__e__
17	se__e__t__en	65	s__xt__-f__v__	600	s__x h__n__re__
18	e__g__t__e__	71	__e__e__ty-__ne	700	__e__en __un__red
19	n__n__t__e__	82	e__g__t__-t__o	800	ei__h__ hu__d__e__
20	t__en__y	89	__i__h__y-__i__e	900	ni__e __un__re__

What's the time?

A. Numbers: the time

1. Look at the pictures below. What's the time? Write the time in numbers.

a.

2:00

b.

c.

d.

e.

f.

g.

h.

i.

2. Match the time in numbers to the time in words.

1. It's two o'clock. d	a. 3:30
2. It's half past three.	b. 5:15
3. It's quarter past nine.	c. 3:55
4. It's ten o'clock.	d. 2:00
5. It's quarter to seven.	e. 6:30
6. It's quarter past five.	f. 9:15
7. It's five to four.	g. 10:00
8. It's six thirty.	h. 6:45

3. Write the time in numbers.

a. It's four o'clock.	4:00	f. It's ten o'clock.	______
b. It's half past five.	5:30	g. It's ten to five.	______
c. It's six o'clock.	______	h. It's half past one.	______
d. It's half past two.	______	i. It's 20 past three.	______
e. It's quarter past one.	______	j. It's quarter to two.	______

4. Write the time in words.

a. 3:00 It's three o'clock.

b. 5:30 It's half past five.

c. 7:00 ______________________________

d. 8:00 ______________________________

e. 1:30 ______________________________

f. 4:30 ______________________________

I get up at 7 o'clock

A. Vocabulary

Match the phrases to the pictures.

have breakfast ~~wake up~~ get up go shopping have a shower

go to bed do my homework start college have dinner

1.

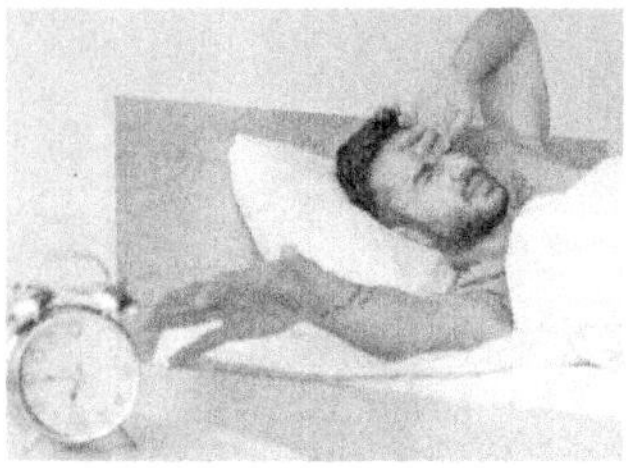

wake up

2.

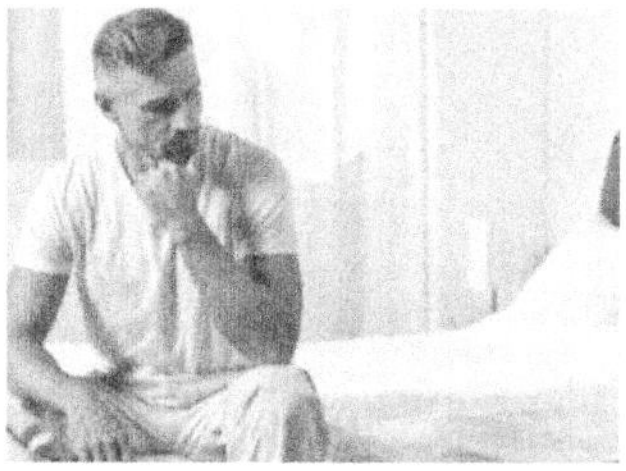

3.

4.

5.

6.

7.

8.

9.

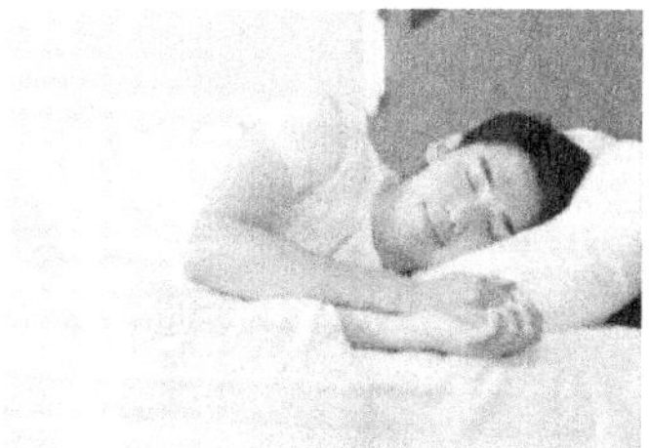

B. Spelling

Fill in the gaps about Mohammad's routine.

I w__ke up at 7 o'cl__ck but I g__t up at 7:15. T__en I ha__e a s__ower. I __ave my __reak__ast at a__out 8 o'cl__ck a__d t__en I go to c__llege by b__s. I s__art c__llege at 9:30 an__ fi__ish cl__ss at 12 o'__lock. A__ter co__lege I go sho__ping and so__etimes I see my frie__ds in t__e ci__y ce__tre. T__en I go h__me a__d I do my h__me__ork. I ha__e din__er at 6 or 7 o'__lock. A__ter dinn__r I c__ean my f__at a__d t__en I re__ax at ho__e. So__etimes I wa__ch TV, s__metimes I wa__ch You Tube vi__eos on my p__one. I go to b__d at a__out 11 o'cl__c__.

C. Writing

Put the words in order to make a sentence. Add capital letters and full stops.

1. up i wake at 7 o'clock

   I wake up at 7 o'clock.

2. get at up i 7:15

   ____

3. have i my breakfast at 8 o'clock about

   ____

4. go bus i by college to

   ____

5. start at college 9:30 i

   ____

6. finish at 12 o'clock i college

   ____

7. college go shopping after i

____

8. get home 4 o'clock about i at

____

9. have i dinner or 6 at o'clock 7

____

10. in i the evening relax

____

11. about at go 11 o'clock i to bed

____

D. Vocabulary

Choose the correct word in each sentence.

1. I usually **get / go** up early.
2. I **wake / get** up at 7 o'clock and I **get / wake** up **to / at** 7:15.
3. After I get up I **have / do** a shower and **then / that** I have my breakfast.
4. I go to college **by / in** bus at 9 o'clock. I **get / go** to college at 9:30.
5. I finish college at 12 o'clock. **After / Before** college I **go to / go** shopping. Then I **go / go to** home and **do / make** my homework.
6. I have my dinner at 6 **and / or** 7 o'clock.
7. I **go bed / go to bed** at about 11 o'clock.

I wake up at 6 o'clock

Writing

1. Use the phrase and write a sentence about yourself. What time do you wake up? What time do you get up?

   a. wake up

   I wake up at 6 o'clock.

   b. get up

   ____

   c. have breakfast

   ____

   d. start college

   ____

   e. finish college

   ____

   f. get home

   ____

   g. have dinner

   ____

   h. go to bed

   ____

I wake up at 6 o'clock

1. What time do you wake up? What time do you have breakfast? Write about your routine.

2. Cover the text and write it again.

3. Cover the texts above and write it again.

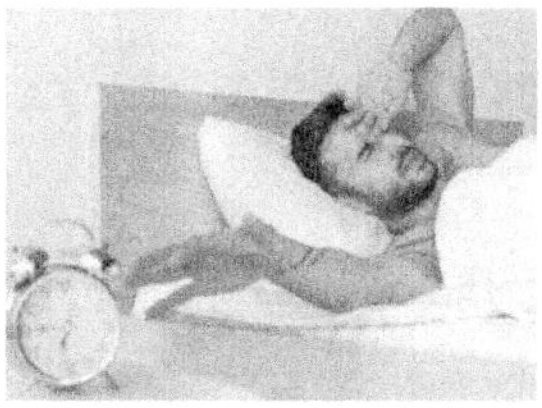

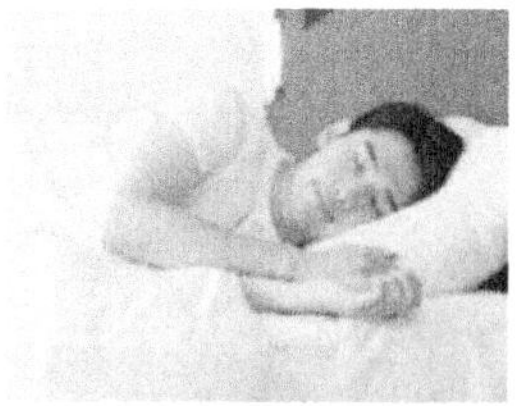

I wake up at five o'clock

Vocabulary and spelling

The words 'wake' and 'five' both finish with **e**. There are more words below which finish with **e**. Find the words and circle them. Some words go down!

~~home~~ ~~like~~ phone five cake cute

time late same drive write

w	r	i	t	e	c	f	l	w	f
o	r	i	h	s	u	n	i	y	r
o	s	h	o	m	e	b	k	l	l
k	f	c	p	c	a	k	e	l	i
i	r	a	p	h	o	n	e	a	n
n	s	w	d	r	i	v	e	t	g
g	c	u	t	e	s	a	m	e	y
t	i	m	e	o	f	i	v	e	m

I wake up at five o'clock

Vocabulary and spelling

Write the answers to the questions in the crossword. Every word finishes with **e**.

1. You can eat this in a café.
2. Your class starts at 9:30 and you get to college at 11 o'clock.
3. You do this in a car.
4. I ________ college, football and TV. They're great!
5. A number after four and before six.
6. You do this in college with a pen or pencil.
7. You can call or text with this.
8. Where you live.
9. – "What's the ________?"
   – "It's 3 o'clock."

e e e e e e e e e e e e e

He's always on time

Grammar: always / never / sometimes / usually

Omid works in a shop. He's a **very good** shop assistant. Circle the correct word.

1. He is **always / never** on time for work.
2. He **always / never** gets up early so that he is **never / usually** late for work.
3. He **usually / never** helps the customers in the shop.
4. He drinks water at work but he **never / sometimes** eats when he's working. He eats his lunch at break time.
5. He's **sometimes / never** rude to the customers. People who go to the shop are **always / never** happy to see him.
6. He **always / sometimes** gives his customers the correct change.
7. He really likes his manager and **sometimes / always** listens to her.
8. He finishes work at 5 o'clock. His manager **sometimes / never** says he can leave early because he **usually / never** works so hard.
9. He **sometimes / never** works extra hours if a workmate is sick. He is paid extra money for this.

I'm usually on time

Spelling

Look-say-cover-write-check

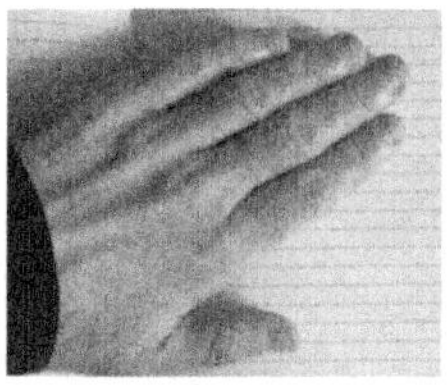

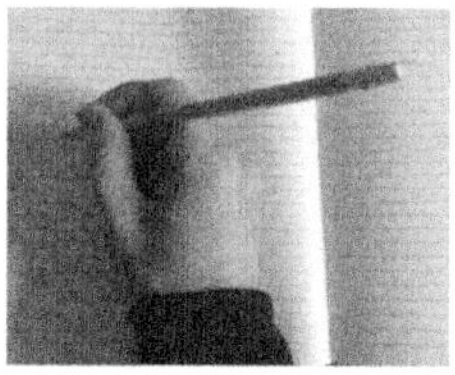

always	___	___	___	___
usually	___	___	___	___
sometimes	___	___	___	___
never	___	___	___	___
homework	___	___	___	___
late	___	___	___	___
on time	___	___	___	___
listen	___	___	___	___
write	___	___	___	___
fight	___	___	___	___
eat	___	___	___	___
phone	___	___	___	___

I'm usually on time

Grammar: always / usually / sometimes / never

What do good students do every day? Use **never / sometimes / usually / always.**

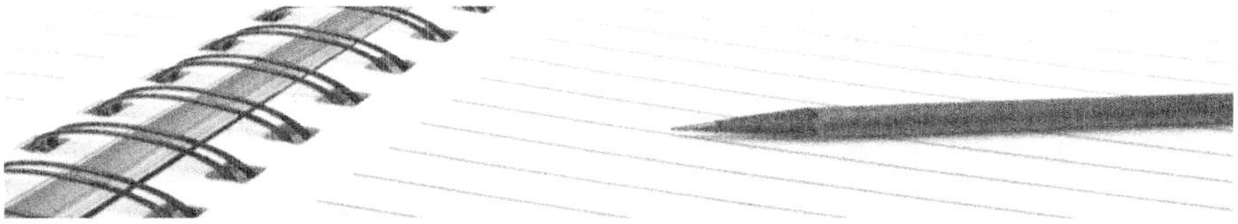

1. on time

   Good students are usually on time.

2. respect their classmates

   ____

3. shout in class

   ____

4. listen to the teacher

   ____

5. do their homework

   ____

6. bring a pencil and paper to class

   ____

7. work hard in class

   ____

8. chat on the phone in class

   ____

I'm usually on time

Writing

1. What do good students do? Write about it.

e.g. Good students are usually on time for class. They usually do their homework.

2. Cover the text and write it again.

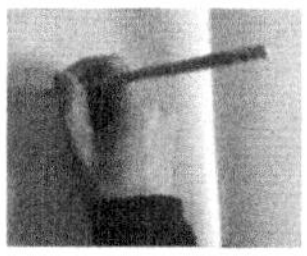

3. Cover the texts above and write it again.

Unit 2

Free time

Free Time

Vocabulary and spelling

Fill in the gaps.

chatting gym music swimming friends cinema
listening games cooking to shopping playing going

1.

I love __________.

2.

I go _______________ every weekend.

3.

I hate _______________.

4.

I love ______________ to ___________.

5.

I love ____________ with my ______________ at the weekend.

6.

I don't like playing _________.

7.

I love ___________ to the ___________.

8.

I love _______________ football with my friends.

9.

I really like going ____ the ______.

I love shopping

Vocabulary and spelling

Look at the hobbies below and then find the words and circle them. Some words go down!

~~football~~ ~~shopping~~ games cooking cinema

swimming music chatting gym

c	m	u	s	i	c	f	c	w	f
o	r	c	h	a	t	t	i	n	g
o	s	f	o	o	t	b	a	l	l
k	f	c	p	o	u	d	t	i	i
i	r	a	p	n	i	n	t	n	n
n	s	w	i	m	m	i	n	g	g
g	c	i	n	e	m	a	n	y	y
w	z	s	g	a	m	e	s	g	m

I like the city centre!

Spelling: words with c

1. Fill in the gaps in the words below. Each word has the letter **c** in it.

a.

I love shopping in the c__ty c__nt__e.

b.

I love c__o__ing! My favourite food is chicken and ric__.

c.

I love going to the c__ne__a but the pr__c__ of a ticket is very expensive.

d.

I always take a book and a pen__ __l to c__ll__ge.

e.

When I go to a c__fe I always have a n__c__ c__p of __ __ffee.

f.

Would you like some ic__ in your ju__c__?

2. Put the letters in order to fill in the gaps. Every word has **c**.

a. I love shopping in the city centre. (itcy / encret)
b. I love a bowl of __________ and a ______ of ____________ for breakfast. (cleaer / upc / fcfoee)
c. I'm going to the ____________ to watch a movie tonight? Do you want to _________ with me? (macine / moce)
d. You can see some changes in the _________ of food. Everything is more expensive. (prcei)
e. I _______ drive but I don't have a _______. (anc / rac)
f. I'm going to _________ chicken and ________ for dinner tonight. (okoc / crei)
g. I always take my books and a __________ to college. (lipenc)
h. Algeria is the biggest _____________ in Africa. (tycrnou)
i. I'm a student. I go to ______________ four days a week. My ____________ starts at 1 o'clock. My teacher is very ________. He helps all the students every day. (geocell / scals / enic)
j. Paris is the _______________ _______ of France. (pacital / ticy)
k. My phone has a great _______________! I love taking photos of my friends. (macera)
l. Sudan is in ___________. (arficA)
m. Would you like some ______ in your orange __________? (eci / jeciu)
n. I always __________ at parties! (denca)

Free time

A. Reading

Read the text about what people in the UK like doing in their free time and do exercises 1 and 2.

People in the UK enjoy about 4 hours of free time every day but what do we like doing after work or college? Our favourite thing we do in our free time is watching TV. 90% of people like TV and many people watch TV for 3 hours a day. That's about 1,000 hours a year! More older people watch TV than young people. Teenagers enjoy apps like You Tube or Tik Tok and love playing games. 27.3% of young people say that gaming is a hobby for them. 60% of people do some exercise sometimes. Some people go to the gym, some people play sport. We like chatting with friends. Many people chat with friends or family for about 30 minutes a day.

1. Match phrases 1 – 7 with a – g. Look at the text above again if you need help.

1. People in the UK enjoy about b
2. Many people watch TV for
3. Our favourite thing we do in our free time is
4. More older people watch TV than
5. Teenagers enjoy apps like
6. 60% of people do
7. Many people chat with friends or family for about

a. 3 hours a day.
b. 4 hours of free time every day.
c. You Tube or Tik Tok.
d. young people.
e. 30 minutes a day.
f. watching TV.
g. some exercise sometimes.

The information above is from www.natcen.ac.uk.

2. Answer the questions.

   a. How many hours of free time do people in the UK have every day?

      People enjoy about 4 hours of free time every day.

   b. What is our favourite thing to do in our free time?

      ____

   c. How many hours of TV do people watch per day?

      ____

   d. Which apps do young people like?

      ____

   e. How many people do exercise?

      ____

   f. How many minutes a day do we spend chatting with friends?

      ____

B. Vocabulary

1. Look at the underlined words in the text. Find a word/phrase which means:

   a. To like something. enjoy

   b. You can see these on your phone, e.g. You Tube, Gmail, Snap Chat. ________________.

   c. Not exactly this number. When we talk about 995 or 1,005, we usually say ____________ 1,000.

   d. We use this word for the thing that you like the most. ____________________

   e. Talking to someone in a friendly way. ____________________

   f. To play sport or go to the gym, for example. ____________________

   g. Young people who are 13 – 19 years old. ____________________

   h. Something that you do in your free time is your _____________. For example, football, gaming, swimming, reading.

   i. At the weekend when you don't work or go to college you have some ____________________.

2. Fill in the gaps.

do some exercise   about (x2)   ~~free time~~   hobby

enjoy   favourite   teenagers   apps   chatting

a. I like going to the gym or watching videos in my free time.

b. I ______________________ every weekend. Sometimes I go swimming, sometimes I play football.

c. I love ________________ with my friends. We meet in a café on Saturday or Sunday.

d. My favourite __________ is football. I play every weekend with my friends.

e. I have lots of great __________ on my phone. I love You Tube and Snap Chat.

f. – How much was your jacket?

– I can't remember the exact price but it was _____________ £30.

g. What do you __________ doing in your free time?

h. I can meet you at just before or maybe just after 1 o'clock tomorrow. Can we meet at _____________ 1 o'clock in a café?

i. There are some ________________ in my class. Isra is 18 years old and Awat is 16 years old.

j. My __________________ food is pizza. I love it!

What's your favourite food?

Write sentences about your favourite things.

hobby app sport food fruit drink

singer movie colour football team place

e.g. My favourite food is chicken and rice.

My favourite hobby is swimming.

1. What's your favourite hobby / app / drink etc? Write it here:

2. Cover the text and write it again.

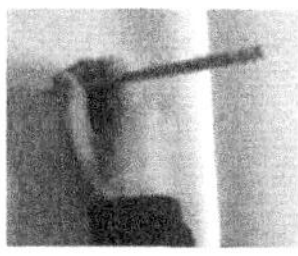

1,000 hours a year

Numbers

Copy and fill in the gaps. In the example, the numbers go up by 50 every time.

e.g. 50, 100,150, 200, 250, 300

a. 100, 200, , 400,

b. 25, 50, , 100, , 150

c. 10, 20, 30, , 50,

d. 5, 10, , 20, , 30,

e. 30, 60, , 120, , 180

f. 150, 300, , 600,

g. 15, 30, , 60, , 90

h. 60, 120, , 240, , 360

i. 80, 160, , 320, 400,

j. 110, 120, , 140, , 160

Everyone is working hard today

Numbers: percentages (%)

There are 10 students in Mohammad's class. Fill in the gaps with a number.

Mohammad

a. 5 of the 10 students are men. 50 %
b. 6 of the students are from Africa. 60 %
c. 4 of the students are from Asia. _____%
d. All of the students like college. _____%
e. 2 students wear glasses. _____%
f. 3 students are not in college today. _____%
g. Everyone does the homework. _____%
h. Nobody was late for class. _____%
i. 2 students are from Iraq. _____%
j. 6 students are from Sudan. _____%
k. 5 students are women. _____%
l. 6 students have black hair. _____%
m. 7 students like cooking. _____%
n. Everyone is working hard today. _____%

Her name is Fatima

Grammar: he / she

1. Circle the correct word.

(a) **Her / His** name (b) **am / is** Fatima. She's been in the UK for 5 years. She (c) **lives / live** in Birmingham now with (d) **his / her** friend Suad. (e) **She / Her** really (f) **likes / like** the people in Birmingham and her college but she (g) **doesn't / don't** like the weather. (h) **He / She** worked in a restaurant in (i) **she / her** country but (j) **she's / I'm** a student now. She (k) **wants / want** to be a chef or a shop assistant when (l) **she / her** English is better. She likes cooking and swimming in her free time. She (m) **goes / go** to her local swimming pool every weekend.

2. Circle the correct word.

(a) **Her / His** name (b) **am / is** Mohamad. (c) **He's / His** a student. (d) **He's / His** from Sudan but he (e) **live / lives** in Scotland. (f) **He's / His** 28 years old. He (g) **go / goes** to college four days a week. He (h) **don't / doesn't** go to class on Fridays. He really likes (i) **he / his** class. He (j) **like / likes** playing football and watching You Tube videos in (k) **he / his** free time.

3. Write about the people. Use the words and pictures to make sentences.

e.g. Ana / student / 23 years old / going to the gym / shopping

Her name is Ana. She's a student. She is 23 years old. She likes going to the gym in her free time. She doesn't like shopping.

a. Ben / student / 27 years old / listening to music / cooking

b. Hong / student / 18 years old / watching videos / gaming

c. Reza / student / 21 years old / going to the gym / swimming

d. Lisa / teacher / 24 years old / tennis / cleaning the kitchen

e. Tuan / student / 17 years old / gaming / housework

Her name is Suad

Write about 3 friends / classmates.

e.g. I have a very good friend. Her name is Suad.
She is from Iraq. She's a student. She is 29 years old.
She likes swimming but she doesn't like football.

1. Write about your friends / classmates.

2. Cover the text above and write this again.

I love playing football!

Writing

1. Put the words in order to make a sentence. Add capital letters and full stops.

   a. love playing i football

   I love playing football.

   b. don't the like i gym

   ____

   c. like really tv i watching

   ____

   d. the kitchen i cleaning hate

   ____

   e. listening music to love i

   ____

   f. we english like learning

   ____

   g. my really shopping like friends

   ____

   h. like i cooking don't

   ____

   i. is washing the dishes OK

   ____

2. What do you like doing in your free time?

e.g. I love playing football. I play football with my friends at the weekend.

Write about two **hobbies** you like doing in your free time:

____

____

____

____

____

3. Which housework do you like? Which housework do you hate?

e.g. I like cleaning the kitchen but I hate cleaning the bathroom.

Now write about **housework** you like / hate:

____

____

____

____

____

____

washing the dishes

doing the laundry

taking out the bin

I'm going shopping

Spelling

Fill in the gaps with **one or two** letters. Use the verbs in brackets.

1. I'm going swimming after college. (swim)
2. What are you ea___ing for dinner tonight? (eat)
3. Do you like ru___ing? It's very good exercise. (run)
4. I really like clea___ing my flat because after I finish it looks so nice. (clean)

5. I love liste___ing to music in the evening. (listen)
6. Be careful when you're cu___ing food as you can easily cut your finger. (cut)
7. We're lear___ing how to spell today. (learn)
8. I like rea___ing my book in the evening. (read)

9. Do you like mee___ing new people? (meet)
10. I love visi___ing my best friend. I see him 3 or 4 days a week. (visit)
11. I love cha___ing with my friends at the weekend. I called three friends yesterday and we cha___ed for hours. (chat)
12. Are you good at pain___ing? (paint)
13. The weather was very bad yesterday. It was rai___ing for hours! (rain)

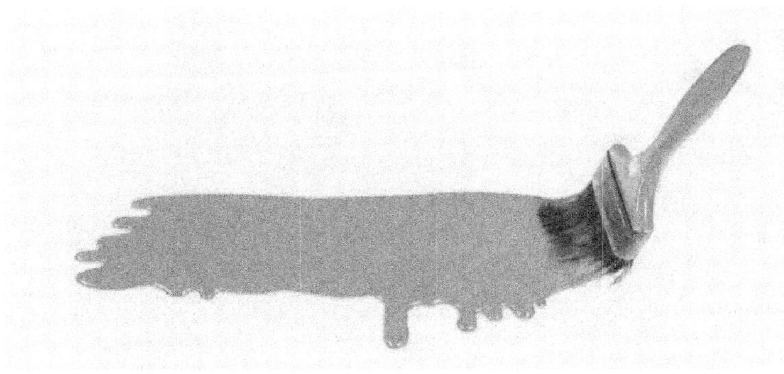

I love music!

Vocabulary and spelling

Fill in the gaps.

guitar ~~listening~~ piano singing ~~music~~ drums dancing play

1.

I love listening to music.

2.

I love ________ at parties.

3.

I like ____________ at parties.

4.

I can play the ________.

5.

I can play the ____________.

6.

I can ________ the ______________.

I can sing

Reading
Read about Hasan and circle the correct answers below. Circle **one or two** answers.

My name is Hasan and I love music. I listen to music every day. I like singing and dancing with my friends. We dance at home. I don't go to night clubs. I can't play the guitar but my friend can play the guitar very well. I like singing and my friends say I can sing very well. My friend plays the guitar and I sing. We like music. I like listening to music from my country and music from many other countries too.

1. Hasan **loves / hates / never listens to** music.
2. He **often / never / sometimes** listens to music.
3. He likes **swimming / singing / dancing** with his friends.
4. He **goes to / doesn't go to / dances in** night clubs.
5. He **can / can't** play the guitar.
6. His friend **can play the / can't play the / has a** guitar.
7. Hasan's friends say that he sings **well / badly**.
8. He likes listening to music from **his country / many countries.**

I can sing

Writing

Copy and write about Hasan.

My name is Hasan and I love
music. I listen to music every day.
I like singing and dancing with
my friends. I can't play the guitar
but my friend can play the
guitar very well. I like singing and
my friends say I can sing very
well. My friend plays the guitar
and I sing. We like music. I like
listening to music from my
country and music from many
other countries too.

I can sing

Writing

Put the words in order to make a sentence about Hasan. Add capital letters and full stops.

1. name is music my and i hasan love

My name is Hasan and I love music.

2. to day i every listen music

3. with like i my singing and dancing friends

4. dance we at home

5. don't i go night clubs to

6. can't i play guitar the

7. my friend very well play the guitar can

8. sing very i well can

9. the guitar plays my friend and i sing

10. listening to music my country from i like

Can you play the piano?

Grammar: can / can't

Fill in the gaps with **can** or **can't** and a verb from below.

can can't	play (x4) swim cook (x2) write run ride drive

1. John's very bad at cooking. He can cook something easy like rice but he can't cook anything more difficult. My dad is an excellent cook! He __________ ________ chicken and rice or pasta so well!
2. I can ride a bike but I __________ ________ a car. I need to get some lessons.

3. Maria __________ ________ the piano very well. She started learning when she was a child. I didn't learn to play any musical instruments at school so I __________ ________ the piano or anything else.
4. My friends __________ ________ but I can't. I'm sad about this because they go to the swimming pool every Sunday. I'm going to learn so that I can go with them.
5. My best friend plays football and she's really good but I __________ ________ football. I'm so bad but I'm good at other sports. I __________ ________ basketball really well.
6. It's not easy for me but I __________ ________ in English if it's something that is not too difficult.
7. I can ride a bike but I __________ ________ a horse. It looks very difficult!
8. Jenny __________ ________ very fast! She wins all the races at her school.

I can ride a bike

Grammar: can / can't

Look at the grammar below. Five of the sentences are correct but five have a mistake. Which sentences are correct? Change the incorrect sentences.

1. I can ride a bike. ✓

2. I can't ~~driving~~ drive a car but I can ride a bike. ✗

3. I can to play football very well. I can play lots of sports.

4. Can you cook? I can cook some meals like pasta or chicken and rice.

5. I can speak English, Arabic and Kurdish. I can read and write in Arabic but I can't read in Kurdish.

6. I can sing but I cant play a musical instrument.

7. Can you ride a horse? I can't ride a horse but I can ride a bike!

8. My friends all like sport. Some of my friends can playing football really well and some can play basketball.

9. Can you reading and writing in English?

10. I can't swim but my friends can swim very well. They go swimming every weekend.

I can sing

Writing

Write a sentence with can or can't. Write about yourself or your friends.

1. 

drive

e.g. My teacher can drive but I can't drive yet.

2. 

swim

3. 

play the piano

4. 

ride a bike

5. 

cook

Unit 3

How's the weather?

The weather

Vocabulary

Fill in the gaps.

sunny cold ~~hot~~ raining storm

windy rainbow cloudy snowing

1. I love hot weather in the summer. I love relaxing in the sun!
2. You're going to need an umbrella today. It's ______________ now and I think it's going to be like this all day!

3. Remember to take a warm jacket, your gloves and hat with you later. It's so ________ today!

4. I didn't sleep well last night because there was a big __________! It was so noisy.
5. Look outside at the beautiful ________________! The colours are amazing! I love it when we can see one when it's sunny after some rain.

6. The sky is so grey today. Where's the sun? I don't like this _______________ weather.
7. Look outside! It's ______________________ just now. Let's go out and play. We can have a snowball fight!
8. It's so ____________ today that I lost my hat and my umbrella is broken now! It was so bad that it was difficult to walk!

9. Look outside! It's really ____________ today. I'm going to wear my sunglasses later.

The Weather

Vocabulary and spelling

Find the words and circle them. Some words go down!

~~hot~~ ~~storm~~ sunny snowing

cloudy raining cold rainbow windy

e	h	c	o	l	d	f	u	w	f
h	r	i	h	s	u	n	n	y	r
s	s	h	o	t	w	r	v	w	a
t	f	c	l	o	u	d	y	i	i
o	r	a	i	n	i	n	g	n	n
r	a	s	a	u	l	e	s	d	b
m	a	m	w	c	n	a	m	y	o
w	z	s	n	o	w	i	n	g	w

The months and the seasons

Reading and vocabulary

A. True or false?

1. There are 12 months. True
2. Each month has 30 days.
3. January is the first month of the year.
4. November is the last month.

5. In the UK, July is in the winter.
6. In the UK, April is in the spring.
7. In the UK, December is cold.
8. April is after May.
9. September is before October.

10. June is between May and July.

B. Answer the questions about the months.

1. What is the 2nd month? February
2. What is the 10th month?

3. What is the 5th month?
4. Which month is after January?
5. Which month is before June?
6. Which month is after September?
7. Name a month which is in the winter in the UK.
8. Name a month which is in the summer in the UK.
9. Name a month which is in the autumn in the UK.
10. Name a month which is in the spring in the UK.

It's cloudy today

Vocabulary and spelling

Write the answers to the questions in the crossword.
Every answer has **ou** or **ow**.

1. A small animal. Sometimes cats kill this animal!
2. Some people live in these. They are like flats but usually bigger.
3. Some people do this when they are angry.
4. You use this to dry yourself after a shower.
5. We get milk and beef from this animal.
6. The opposite of quiet.
7. The colour of chocolate and trees.
8. The opposite of inside.
9. When it's 3:02 many people say, "It's ___________ 3 o'clock."
10. The opposite of up.
11. The opposite of north.
12. - "______ are you?"
    - "I'm fine."

Greece

Writing

Copy the text and write about Greece.

My name is Ana and I live in
Greece. Greece is a very hot
country. It is so hot in the
summer. It's very hot here but
we have some rain sometimes
and it is a bit cold in winter. I like
sunny days in Greece. I go to the
beach when it is sunny if I'm not
busy. The only problem here is
when it's too hot.

Vietnam

Reading

Read about Tuan and circle the correct answer below.

Circle **one or two** answers.

My name is Tuan and I'm from Vietnam but I live in Aberdeen now. I'm from the capital city, Hanoi. Vietnam is a very hot country. It is very hot in the summer. Sometimes it is too hot for me! It is very hot from April to September. We have more rain when it is hot. We have storms sometimes with so much rain. It is not so hot for the rest of the year. I like the weather in Vietnam when it is not so hot. I live in Aberdeen now. It's very cold for me here in the winter but I like the summer.

1. His name is **Tony / Tuan**.
2. Tuan is from **Aberdeen / Vietnam** but he lives in **Aberdeen / Vietnam** now.
3. Vietnam is **a bit / very hot** in the summer.
4. It is hot for **five / six** months.
5. There is more rain when it is **hot / cold**.
6. Vietnam **never / sometimes** has storms.
7. Tuan **doesn't like / loves** very hot weather.
8. He likes the **summer / winter** in Aberdeen.

Vietnam

Writing

Put the words in order. Add capital letters and full stops.

1. name is my tuan i'm from and vietnam

My name is Tuan and I'm from Vietnam.

2. is vietnam a very country hot

3. from april it's very hot to september

4. sometimes it is hot too

5. like hot i don't very weather

6. have we storms sometimes

7. i live Aberdeen now in

8. i the summer like in aberdeen

9. i in aberdeen like don't the winter

Vietnam

Punctuation

1. Can you see some mistakes with capital letters and full stops in the text about Tuan?

M T
~~m~~y name is ~~t~~uan / and i'm from Vietnam but I live in aberdeen now I'm from the capital city, hanoi. vietnam is a very hot . country it is very hoT from April to september. I like the Weather . in vietnam when it is not so Hot

2. Answer the questions below with a sentence about yourself. Be careful with capital letters and full stops.

   e.g. When is your country hot? Which months?

   Egypt is hot from June to September.

   a. What's your name? Where are you from?

   ___

   b. Where do you live?

   ___

   c. Where do you go to study English?

   ___

   d. When is your country hot? Which months?

   ___

   e. When is your country cold? Which months?

   ___

The months

Vocabulary

Copy the words. Write every month three times.

e.g. January January January

February

March

April

May

June

July

August

September

October

November

December

The weather

Spelling

Look-cover-say-write-check

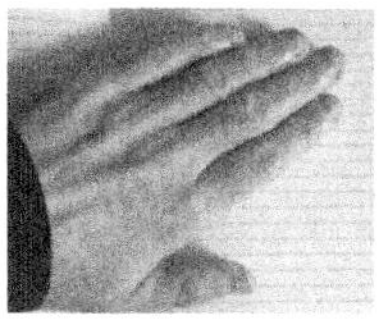 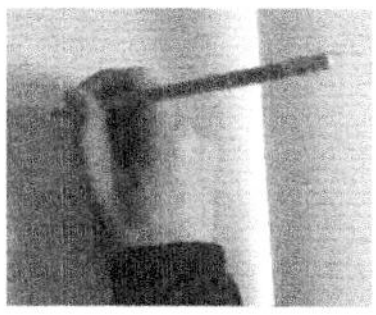

cold	________	________	________	________
country	________	________	________	________
people	________	________	________	________
days	________	________	________	________
rain	________	________	________	________
when	________	________	________	________
sunny	________	________	________	________
some	________	________	________	________
months	________	________	________	________
summer	________	________	________	________
winter	________	________	________	________
spring	________	________	________	________
autumn	________	________	________	________

The weather

Writing

How's the weather where you live just now? And in your country now?

e.g. My name is Mohammed. I am from Syria but I live in Blackburn. It is hot in Blackburn today but it's very hot in Syria.

1. Write about the weather where you live now and in your country:

2. Cover the text and write it again.

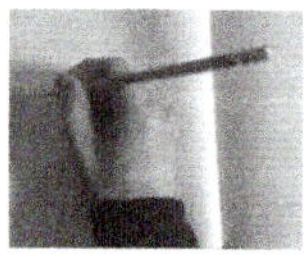

When it's hot….

Grammar: the present simple

Fill in the gaps with the correct form of the word in brackets.

1. When it's sunny I always __go__ outside. (go)
2. When it's raining I ________ at home and ________ TV. I don't like getting wet! (stay / watch)
3. When it's snowing my friend Sue always ________ in the snow with her kids. (play)
4. When it's hot I ________ my friends and we ____ to the park (meet / go).
5. I know that you _______ tea but I didn't know that you _________ coffee. (like / drink)
6. My friend ______ a car and she sometimes __________ to college. (have / drive)
7. I ________ to college but my best friend _______ to college by bus. (walk / go)
8. My friend ________ in a house and she _____ a lovely garden. (live / have)
9. In my class we _______ and __________ every day. (read / write)
10. Our teacher ________ us with our English every day. She ____ a very good teacher. (help / be)
11. My friend is a student. He ________ to college 4 days a week and __________ hard. (go / work)
12. Our teacher __________ us homework every day. Most of the students ____ the homework but I ______________ to do it sometimes. (give / do / forget)

When it's raining....

Writing

What do you do when it's hot? What do you do when it's cold / snowing / raining?

e.g. My name is Sara. When it is hot I go to the park. When it's cold and it's raining I still go to college but I go home after my class. At the weekend I go shopping when it's cold or it's raining.

1. Write your answer:

2. Cover the text and write it again.

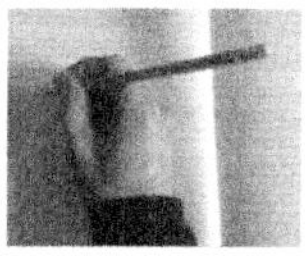

How's the weather?

Vocabulary and spelling

The word 'weather' has **th** in it. Look at the words with **th** in them below. Find the words and circle them. Some words go down!

~~then~~ ~~this~~ the think thing thanks

there with that weather month them

e	h	c	t	h	e	n	u	x	w
t	h	e	m	o	n	t	h	g	e
s	t	h	i	n	g	t	v	u	a
t	h	a	t	o	u	h	y	t	t
o	i	a	k	n	i	i	g	h	h
r	s	s	a	u	l	n	s	e	e
m	a	t	h	a	n	k	s	r	r
w	i	t	h	e	r	t	h	e	m

How's the weather?

Vocabulary and spelling

Put the letters in order to make a word. Every word has **th**. Which word needs a capital letter?

1. I think English is difficult sometimes. (kinth)
2. I get up at 7 o'clock and ________ I have a shower. (hent)
3. __________ you for your help. (ahnkt)
4. In my city ___________ are some great cafes and restaurants. (hteer)
5. I had tea and toast for breakfast ________ morning. (hist)
6. Do you go to college in the morning or ______ afternoon? (het)
7. Do you like tea ________ milk? (htiw)
8. I love hot ______________ (theawer)
9. My favourite ________ is June. (mthon)
10. I take the same _________ to college every day. I put water, my books, a pencil and some food in my bag. (tnisgh)

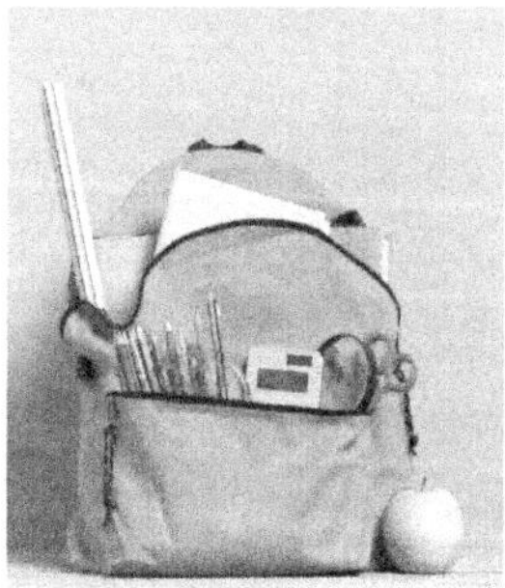

Unit 4

It's a beautiful world

Nature

Vocabulary and spelling

Write the answers to the questions in the crossword.

1. A very big animal with a long trunk (this animal's nose!).
2. You can climb these. There are some very big ones, e.g. Mount Everest, K2, the Himalayas.
3. This is a very small animal. They like cheese and have a long tail. Sometimes cats kill this animal!
4. This animal is very funny and eats bananas.
5. This animal has no legs and some are very dangerous.
6. You can relax here. It is a place near the sea.
7. We get milk and beef from this animal.
8. A _______ has 8 legs. Some people are scared of these.
9. This animal has two wings and it can fly.

Nature

Vocabulary

Fill in the gaps.

beach cows ~~mouse~~ mountains
snakes spiders elephant birds monkeys

1. There was a __mouse__ in my garden yesterday. It was very small with a very long tail.
2. My friend lives near a beautiful ____________. I visited her last year and we had a great day. We went sunbathing and I enjoyed swimming in the sea!
3. There are so many beautiful _________________ in my country. Some people climb up one and enjoy the view at the top.
4. There are some dangerous _____________ in my country. Some of them are small but some are more than one metre long.
5. I hate _______________. When I see one in the shower I'm always so scared.
6. I see so many _____________ in my garden every day. I can hear them singing when I wake up in the morning sometimes.
7. I saw a very big ______________ in the zoo last year. It had very big ears and a long trunk. It was beautiful! I love seeing the _________________ too. I love seeing them jump from tree to tree.
8. I worked on a farm about five years ago. We had sheep, chickens and ___________.

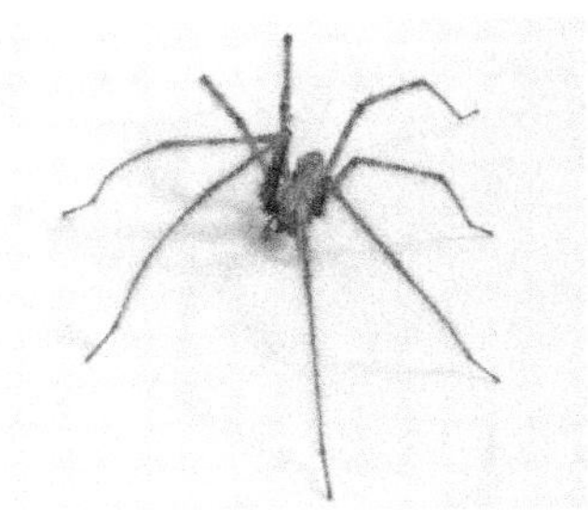

Cheetahs are very fast!

mice

Vocabulary: adjectives

Circle the correct adjective. Choose **one or two** words.

1. Mice are so **small / dangerous / fast.**
2. Elephants are very **small / big / beautiful**.
3. Some snakes are very **cute / dangerous / small**.
4. Ah, look at that puppy. He's so **small / cute / slow**.
5. Snails are very **dangerous / slow / fast**.
6. Lions are **dangerous / slow / fast**.
7. Cheetahs are very **slow / fast / dangerous**.
8. Crocodiles are very **cute / dangerous / small**.
9. Mosquitoes are very **small / big / dangerous**.
10. Sharks are very **dangerous / slow / fast**.

a puppy

a snail

a cheetah

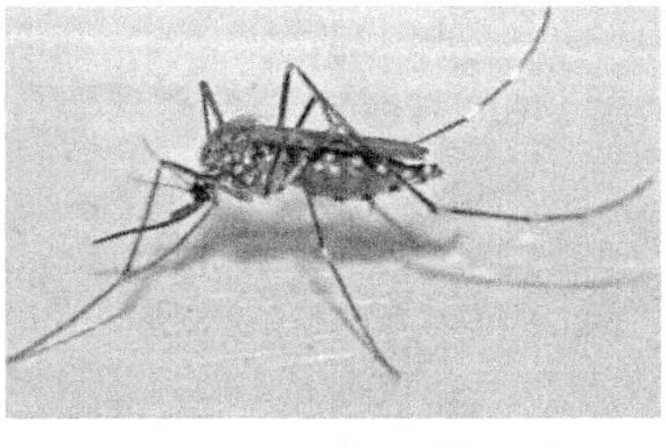

a mosquito

a crocodile

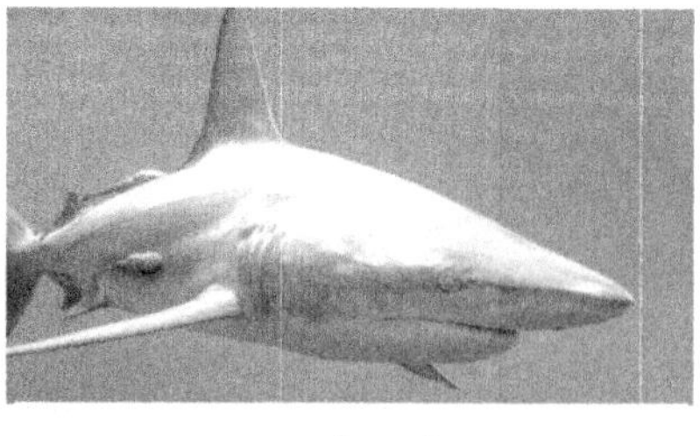

a shark

My country

Writing

Copy the text and write about Susan.

My name is Susan and I am
from Wales. Wales is a beautiful
country. We have lots of
fantastic mountains and many
beautiful beaches. You can see
animals in farms or zoos. We
don't have dangerous animals
but you can see lions or tigers in
the zoos. Many people have pet
cats or dogs. I have a pet dog.
His name is Bobby and he's so
cute. He's part of the family!

My country

Vocabulary

Look at the underlined words in the text.

My name is Susan and I am from Wales. Wales is a beautiful country. We have lots of fantastic mountains and many beautiful beaches. You can see animals in farms or zoos. You can see cows or sheep in the countryside. We don't have dangerous animals but you can see lions or tigers in the zoos. Many people have pet cats or dogs. I have a pet dog. His name is Bobby and he's so cute. He's part of the family!

Which word / phrase means:

1. We get beef and milk from this animal. cows
2. Very. so
3. Animals which we can use to make a jumper or scarf. ____________
4. If an animal can hurt or kill you it is ________________________.
5. An animal that lives with people in our homes. __________
6. A place where people go to see animals like lions, tigers and monkeys. People like seeing the animals and learning about them. ____________
7. Many. ________________
8. A place where you can see chickens, cows, sheep etc. These places sell food and drink like meat, eggs and milk to shops. _____________
9. Ah! Look at the baby! She's so _________!
10. Very good. ___________________
11. An area outside a city. You can see farms here. ______________________
12. For example, a person or place that looks really nice. ___________________

My country

Writing

Copy the sentences but add spaces. Add capital letters and full stops.

1. mynameissusanandI'mfromwales

   My name is Susan and I'm from Wales.

2. walesisabeautifulcountry

   ____

3. wehavemanybeautifulbeaches

   ____

4. youcanseeanimalsinfarms

   ____

5. youcanseecowsinthecountryside

   ____

6. wedon'thavedangerousanimals

   ____

7. manypeoplehavepetcatsordogs

   ____

8. ihaveapetdog

   ____

9. he'ssocute

   ____

10. he'spartofthefamily

    ____

My country

Vocabulary and spelling

The words below are all in the text about Susan.
Find the words and circle them.

~~pet~~ beautiful visit country animals

places beaches dogs cats farms

b	e	a	c	h	e	s	y	g	m
e	c	o	u	n	t	r	y	e	a
a	n	i	m	a	l	s	l	h	e
u	p	f	a	r	m	s	e	p	p
t	b	a	y	e	d	u	e	l	c
i	a	x	u	s	t	x	u	a	a
f	d	t	c	h	p	e	t	c	t
u	u	d	n	d	o	g	s	e	s
l	s	g	v	i	s	i	t	s	b

Bolivia

A. Reading

Read about Bolivia and answer the questions below.

My name is Alicia and I am from Bolivia. Bolivia is a beautiful country. You can visit so many beautiful places. We have so many amazing mountains and a famous lake. Many people come to Bolivia to see Lake Titicaca and the Amazon jungle too. You can see many beautiful animals here. We have many llamas like the one in this photo. They are very friendly! You can also see lots of beautiful birds. If you visit the Amazon jungle you can see monkeys and dangerous animals like snakes, and crocodiles. There are some dangerous spiders too. You can also see the famous pink river dolphin. Some people swim with the dolphins in the Amazon River! It's amazing but I don't want to swim with them!

What can you see in Bolivia? Tick or cross the sentences.

1. A beautiful country. ✔
2. One or two beautiful places. ✘
3. Lots of great mountains.
4. Many visitors.
5. Lake Titicaca, a famous lake.
6. A famous jungle.
7. Some dangerous animals.
8. Black river dolphins.
9. People swimming with dolphins.
10. Alicia swimming with a dolphin.

The Amazon jungle

a pink river dolphin

Lake Titicaca

B. Vocabulary

Match the pictures to the words in the text about Alicia.

crocodile mountains monkey lake

spider dolphin snake bird jungle

1. 

____

2. 

____

3. 

____

4. 

____

5. 

____

6. 

____

7. 

____

8. 

____

9. 

____

C. Reading

Read the text again and answer these questions.

1. True or false?

a. Alicia is from Bolivia. True
b. There are no nice places to see in Bolivia.
c. Alicia is very scared of llamas.
d. Some animals can hurt you in Bolivia.
e. Alicia swims with the dolphins sometimes.
f. Alica loves her country.

2. Fill in the gaps.

animals ~~country~~ lots people but swim some see friendly

My name is Alicia and I am from Bolivia. Bolivia is a beautiful (a) country. You can visit so many beautiful places. We have so many amazing mountains and a famous lake. Many (b) ______________ come to Bolivia to see Lake Titicaca and the Amazon jungle too. You can (c) ______ many beautiful animals here. We have many llamas like the one in this photo. They are very (d) ________________! You can see (e) ________ of beautiful birds . If you visit the Amazon jungle you can see monkeys and dangerous (f) ___________ like snakes, and crocodiles. There are (g) _________ dangerous spiders too. You can also see the famous pink river dolphin. Some people (h) _______ with the dolphins in the Amazon River! It's amazing (i) ______ I don't want to swim with them!

The Amazon jungle

Lake Titicaca is amazing!

Writing

People who see Lake Titicaca say that it is amazing! Do you know some amazing places? Which animals can you see there?

e.g. I live in Glasgow. You can see a famous lake near Glasgow. It's name is Loch Lomond and it is beautiful. I am from Egypt. The pyramids are amazing. You can see some beautiful animals. You can see camels and birds.

1. Write about amazing places that you know:

2. Cover the text above and write this again.

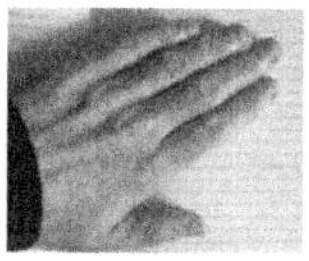

Can I take a photo?

Spelling: f and ph

The letters **f** and **ph** often sound the same. Fill in the gaps below with **f** or **ph**. Can you read the words?

1. I'm __f__rom __F__rance but I live in London now.
2. – What's your ___avourite ___ood?

   – I love ___ish and chips!
3. I went to a zoo last week with some ___riends. It was great! We saw ele___ants and dol___ins!
4. I was sick last week so I went to the ___armacy and got some tablets.
5. What's your ___avourite ___ruit? I love oranges and bananas.
6. I have a great camera on my ___one. I can take ___antastic ___otos sometimes.
7. What time do you start and ___inish college?
8. I was a ___armer in my country. We had sheep, cows and chickens on the ____arm.
9. There are 26 letters in the English al___abet.
10. My friend has a lovely garden ___ull of beautiful ___lowers.
11. I'm going to Turkey by plane tomorrow. My __light is at 10 o'clock.
12. I've been in the UK ___or ___ive years.

What a beautiful flower!

Vocabulary and spelling: f and ph

Find the words and circle them.

~~fruit~~ phone pharmacy farmer fish alphabet

elephant photo five dolphin flower from

e	p	e	f	r	u	i	t	y	p
l	h	c	p	h	o	t	o	y	f
e	a	p	h	o	n	e	g	l	r
p	r	c	f	a	r	m	e	r	o
h	m	f	l	o	w	e	r	c	m
a	a	c	x	f	i	s	h	a	a
n	c	a	r	r	e	r	e	t	c
t	y	d	o	l	p	h	i	n	y
g	a	l	p	h	a	b	e	t	x

A litre of water

Numbers: how much?

Fill in the gaps.

kilometre stone metres ~~litre~~ kilometres
inch pint grammes miles kilogrammes

1. A big bottle of water has 1 __litre__ of water in it.
2. The speed limit in town and cities in the UK is usually 20 or 30 __________ per hour.
3. There are 1,000 metres in a __________________.
4. 1 ________ is about 2.5cm.
5. I weigh 75 _____________________, which is about 12 stone.
6. My friend is very tall. He's over 6 foot tall. That's nearly 2 __________.
7. You can buy a ________ of beer in pubs in the UK. That's just over half a litre.
8. It's about 200 miles from London to Manchester by car. That's over 300 ____________________.
9. There are 1,000 ___________ in a kilogramme.
10. Donkeys weigh nearly 200kg or 30 ________.

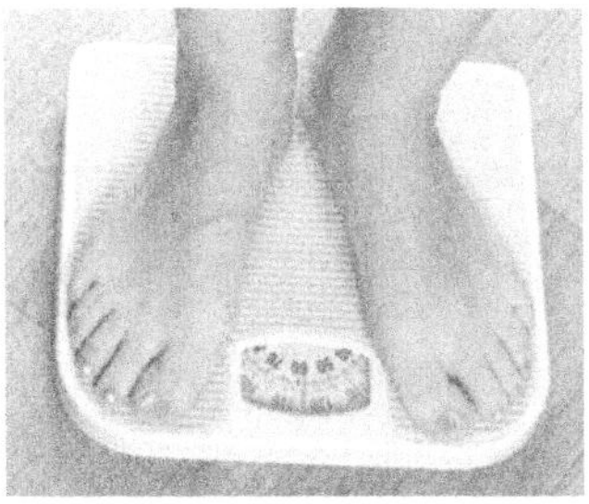

a donkey

Unit 5

What's the matter?

The body

Vocabulary

Tick the correct word.

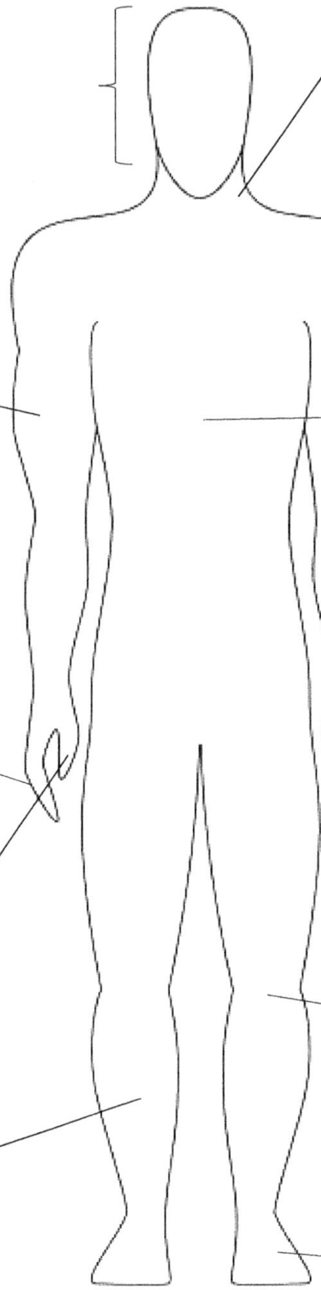

1. ☐ shoulder
   ☑ head
   ☐ hand

2. ☐ shoulder
   ☐ arm
   ☐ hand

3. ☐ foot
   ☐ finger
   ☐ thumb

4. ☐ foot
   ☐ thumb
   ☐ finger

5. ☐ leg
   ☐ shoulder
   ☐ foot

6. ☐ head
   ☐ neck
   ☐ back

7. ☐ stomach
   ☐ knee
   ☐ shoulder

8. ☐ stomach
   ☐ thumb
   ☐ shoulder

9. ☐ head
   ☐ arm
   ☐ hand

10. ☐ finger
    ☐ knee
    ☐ foot

11. ☐ leg
    ☐ arm
    ☐ foot

I'm sick

Vocabulary

1. Tick the correct word / phrase.

a.

☑ cold
☐ headache
☐ cough

b.

☐ tablets
☐ plaster
☐ cream

c.

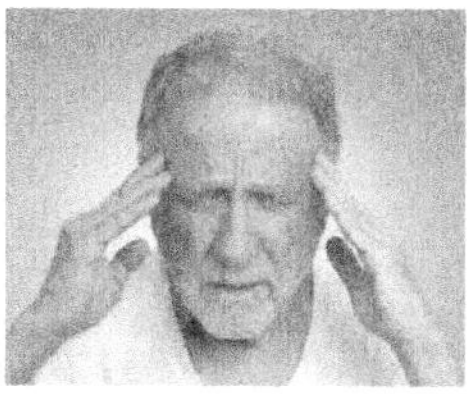

☐ cold
☐ headache
☐ cough

d.

☐ toothache
☐ cough
☐ cream

e.

☐ cream
☐ plaster
☐ cold

f.

☐ My back hurts.
☐ headache
☐ cough

g.

☐ toothache
☐ headache
☐ cough

h.

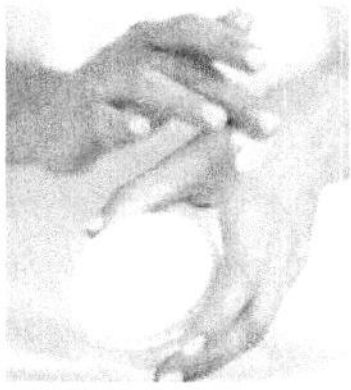

☐ toothache
☐ cream
☐ tablets

i.

☐ medicine
☐ headache
☐ cream

2. Fill in the gaps.

tablets ~~cream~~ plaster medicine

toothache hurts broken cold cough

a. My back hurts! At the pharmacy they gave me some __cream__ and it's really good. It still hurts but I'm feeling better.

b. I have a very bad ________. I need to blow my nose! Do you have a tissue?

c. - I have very bad ________________.

- You should go to the dentist.

d. Do you have a ______________? I've cut my finger!

e. I didn't go to college for three weeks. I had an accident and my leg was __________.

f. I have a really bad headache. At the pharmacy they gave me these ______________. I take two every four hours.

g. Ow! My back really ___________! I'm going to the GP tomorrow.

h. - That sounds like you have a very bad ___________! Would you like some water or honey and lemon tea?

- No thanks. I got some ______________ from the pharmacy. I take two teaspoons every four hours.

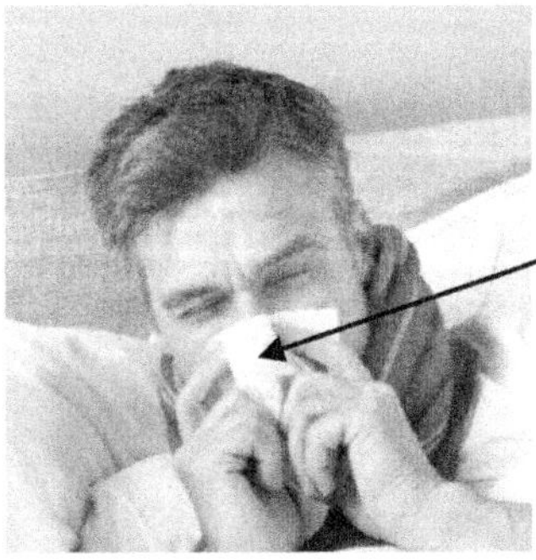

a tissue

He's blowing his nose.

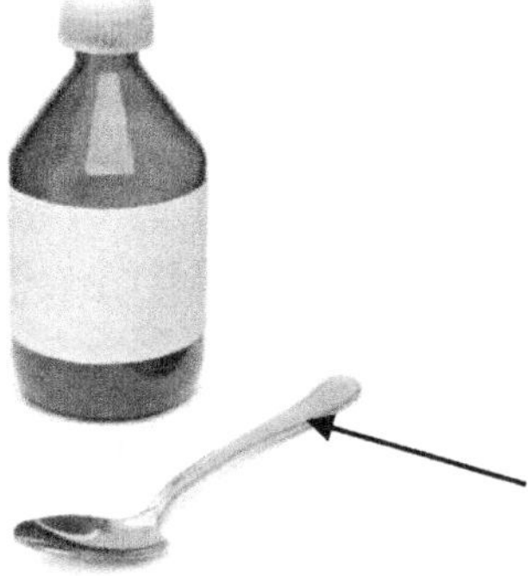

a teaspoon

When I'm sick

Reading
Read about Claire and circle the correct word for numbers 1 – 7 below. Circle **one or two** words / phrases.

My name is Claire. When I'm sick I usually stay at home and rest. I sometimes have medicine or tablets but not every time. I never go to work when I am very sick. If I'm very sick I always go to the pharmacy or the GP. I was sick last week. I had very bad flu. I didn't go to work for three days. I had some medicine and went to bed to get some rest. I feel better now.

1. When Claire is sick she usually **stays at home / rests / goes to work**.
2. She **never / sometimes / always** has tablets.
3. She **goes / doesn't go / never goes** to work when she's very sick.
4. She goes to **the pharmacy / the GP / work** every time she's very sick.
5. She was sick **last week / last month / last year**. She had **toothache / the flu / stomachache**.
6. She didn't go to work for **2 days / 3 days / a week**. She **went to bed / had some medicine / went to work** when she was sick.
7. She **is sick / feels fine / feels bad** now.

When I'm sick

Writing

Copy the sentences but add spaces. Add capital letters and full stops.

1. iusuallystayathomeandrest

   I usually stay at home and rest.

2. isometimeshavetablets

   ____

3. igotobedandsleepallday

   ____

4. inevergotocollegewheniamverysick

   ____

5. iwassicklastweek

   ____

6. iwenttobed

   ____

7. ihadsomemedicine

   ____

8. ifeelbetternow

   ____

When I'm sick

Vocabulary and spelling

Find the words from the text about Amina in the Student's Book. Find the words and circle them.

~~give~~ when every hospital broken

always sick sleep sometimes hurt

s	o	m	e	t	i	m	e	s
d	j	h	u	r	t	b	e	l
t	c	i	k	e	r	r	w	m
f	g	i	v	e	e	o	h	n
s	l	e	e	p	z	k	e	s
a	l	w	a	y	s	e	n	i
g	o	z	e	g	y	n	n	c
h	o	s	p	i	t	a	l	k
s	e	v	e	r	y	x	g	d

I usually have honey and lemon tea

A. Grammar: always / sometimes / usually / never

Sentences 1 - 6 are possible ideas if you are sick. Circle the correct adverb of frequency.

1. When I'm sick I **always / sometimes** go to the pharmacy but sometimes I just go to bed and rest.
2. I **always / usually** have honey and lemon tea when I'm sick. I do this every time I'm sick because I always feel better.
3. I **always / sometimes** go to hospital if I have a very bad accident. You need to see a nurse or a doctor.
4. I **always / never** go to the dentist when I have toothache. I have a very good dentist. She helps me every time I have toothache.
5. I'm **never / usually** sick in the winter, maybe for a week or so. I usually get a cold or cough.
6. I **always / sometimes** take tablets when I have a headache but sometimes I just drink water or go to bed and I don't take any tablets.

B. Writing

What do you do when you're sick?

____

____

____

____

____

____

____

____

I have a sore throat

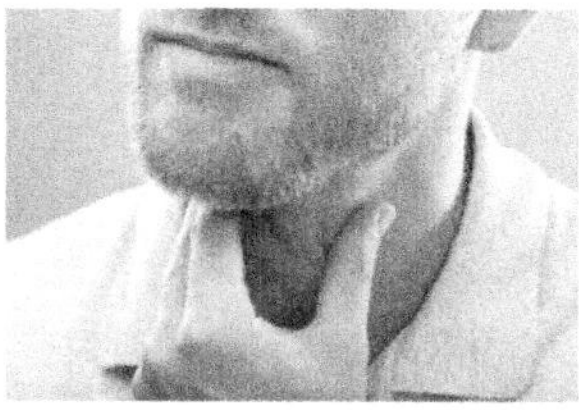

Vocabulary and spelling

The word 'throat' has **oa** in it. Many **oa** and **ow** words sound the same. Look at some more words below that have **oa** and **ow**. Find the words and circle them.

~~soap~~	~~goal~~	window	boat	bowl	yellow	coach	snow
know	coat	show	goat	below	grow	road	slow

w	i	n	d	o	w	m	e	s	g
g	j	k	u	r	b	o	w	l	r
o	c	n	k	e	r	k	y	c	o
a	s	o	a	p	b	r	e	o	w
l	l	w	e	r	o	o	l	a	c
a	o	w	g	o	a	t	l	c	o
g	w	z	e	a	t	e	o	h	a
s	h	o	w	d	o	w	w	k	t
b	e	l	o	w	i	s	n	o	w

I have a sore throat

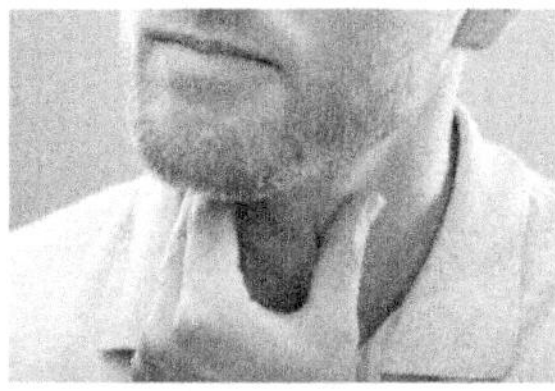

Vocabulary and spelling

The word 'throat' has **oa** in it. Many **oa** and **ow** words sound the same. Put the letters in order to make a word. Every word has **ow** or **oa**.

1. I love ___boat___ trips. They are very relaxing. (toba)
2. Take ________ and shampoo to the pool if you want a shower after we go swimming later. (opas)
3. Look out the ___________. It's __________! Put your ________ on if you go outside. We can have a snowball fight! (winwod / nowsing / toca)

4. I like ___________ or a ________ of cereal for breakfast. (tosta / blow)
5. I usually go to Sheffield by train but I'm going there by _________ tomorrow. It's slow but it's cheaper. (choca)
6. My favourite colour is ___________. (owelly)
7. Do you ________ all the answers to these questions? (wonk)
8. You can get milk from cows or _________. (stoga)

9. The opposite of 'fast' is '_________.' (owls)
10. I watched my friend playing football at the weekend and he scored a great _________! (loga)
11. Can I ________ you my homework please teacher? Can you check it for me please? (owsh)

What's your address?

Writing

Can you write your address? Try not to copy. Write it two times.

Name	....
Address	....
Post code	....
DOB	....
Tel. no.	....
e-mail	....

Name	....
Address	....
Post code	....
DOB	....
Tel. no.	....
e-mail	....

Dates

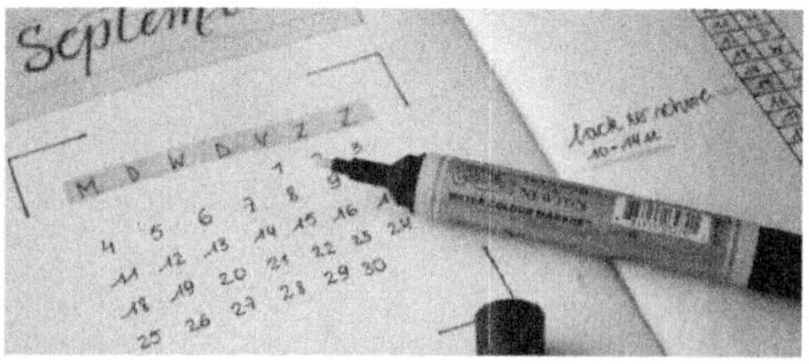

Numbers: dates

Fill in the gaps.

1. The 1st of March 2005 — 01/____/05
2. The 5th of May 2012 — ____/05/12
3. The 17th of October 2011 — 17/10/____
4. The 14th of December 2001 — ____/____/01
5. The 28th of July 1990 — 28/____/90
6. The 19th of February 2017 — ____/02/____
7. The 4th of April 2010 — 04/____/10
8. The 26th of January 2001 — 26/____/____
9. The 3rd of October 1999 — ____/____/99
10. The 11th of November 1998 — 11/____/____
11. The 7th of June 2004 — ____/____/____
12. The 10th of August 2015 — ____/____/____
13. The 19th of December 2023 — ____/____/____
14. The 21st of April 1995 — ____/____/____
15. The 22nd of May 2002 — ______________
16. The 4th of March 2022 — ______________
17. The 3rd of October 2010 — ______________
18. The 1st of July 2008 — ______________
19. The 10th of February 1980 — ______________
20. The 2nd of January 1995 — ______________

Dates

Numbers: dates

Fill in the gaps.

1.	04/09/09	The 4th of September 2009
2.	02/02/14	The ____ of February ________
3.	02/09/13	The ____ of ________________ 2013
4.	17/12/14	The 17th of December _________
5.	09/10/92	The ____ of October 1992
6.	19/08/22	The 19th of _____________ 2022
7.	11/04/06	The _____ of April _________
8.	26/02/02	______ 26th of ________________ 2002
9.	03/10/23	The ____ of October _________
10.	11/05/98	______ 11th of _________ 1998
11.	16/06/15	The _____ of June _________
12.	04/07/08	______ _____ of ________ 2008
13.	01/01/24	The ____ of ______________ _________
14.	13/07/95	The ________ of _________ 1995
15.	06/03/85	________________________________
16.	05/09/02	________________________________
17.	03/11/21	________________________________
18.	02/07/92	________________________________
19.	01/03/80	________________________________
20.	04/05/19	________________________________

How do you feel?

Vocabulary

Tick the correct word.

1.

☐ happy
☑ scared
☐ hot

2.

☐ hot
☐ sad
☐ cold

3.

☐ sick
☐ happy
☐ angry

4.

☐ happy
☐ angry
☐ cold

5.

☐ hot
☐ hungry
☐ cold

6.

☐ sick
☐ hot
☐ tired

7.

☐ hungry
☐ scared
☐ tired

8.

☐ sick
☐ hungry
☐ scared

9.

☐ sick
☐ tired
☐ angry

I’m happy!

Vocabulary and spelling
Write the answers to the questions in the crossword. Every word is a feeling, e.g. happy, sad, tired.

1. → Maybe you have a cough or a cold. You’re not well.
1. ↓ You can feel this if you see a dangerous animal.
2. How do you feel in the winter?
3. The opposite of happy.
4. The child wanted an ice cream but his mum said “no.” He started shouting and got very ___________.
5. → The opposite of sad.
5. ↓ When you don’t eat for a long time you are ___________.
6. The opposite of cold.
7. You feel like this if you get no sleep.

I'm happy!

Vocabulary: adjectives

1. Fill in the gaps.

scared happy angry sad hot tired ~~sick~~ cold hungry

a. I'm so sick that I'm going to the GP.
b. I'm very __________ because I'm going to a party tonight.
c. Can you close the window please? I'm very ________.
d. You look very ________. What's the problem? Why are you crying? I hope you're OK.
e. I didn't eat any breakfast so I'm very ____________ now.
f. I'm very ____________ of snakes.
g. I had very little sleep last night so I'm so __________ now.
h. I'm so ________. Can you open the window please?
i. Calm down! Why are you shouting? You look so ___________. What's happened?

2. Fill in the gaps with **am, is or are**.

a. I ____ so happy today because it's very sunny outside.
b. ______ you scared of snakes?
c. Why ____ your friend tired? Did she go to bed very late?
d. We ______ hungry. Do you have any food?
e. I ____ very hot. Can you open the window please?
f. My teacher ____ happy when we do the homework.

I'm happy because ...

Writing

How are you today? Why?

e.g. I'm not tired today because I went to bed early. I'm happy because I'm going to see my friends tonight.

1. Write about yourself. How are you today? Why?

2. Cover the text above and write this again.

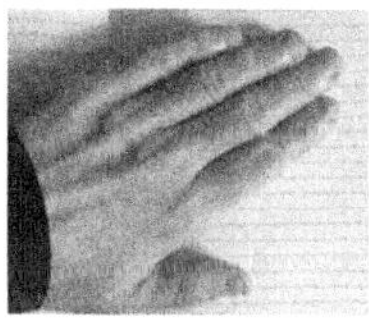

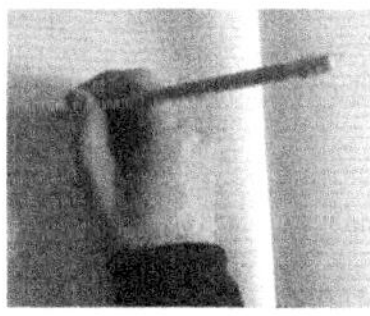

Signs

1. 

2. 

3. 

4. 

5. 

6. 

7. 

Vocabulary

Look at signs 1-7 and match them to sentences a - n. Use some numbers two times.

a. Go here for some information. 7
b. I need the toilet.
c. I have had a bad accident so I need to see a doctor.
d. Please don't smoke here.
e. You can leave the college here.
f. The cafe is open now.
g. Don't drive your car down this road.
h. No smoking.
i. You can go inside the shop. It's not closed.
j. Look for this sign at the hospital if you have an accident.
k. Look for this sign at the bus station if you need help with bus times.
l. No entry.
m. Go here at break time maybe.
n. When class finishes, look for this sign to leave the college.

You can't smoke here

Grammar: can / can't

Circle **can** or **can't**. What can you do in college?

1. You **can / can't** smoke in college.
2. You **can / can't** text your friends in class.
3. Students **can / can't** be late for class.
4. You **can / can't** drink water in class but you **can / can't** eat.
5. Students **can / can't** eat at break time.
6. You **can / can't** ask the teacher to repeat something if you don't understand.
7. You **can / can't** miss lots of classes.
8. Students **can / can't** fight in class.
9. You **can / can't** shout in class.
10. Students **can / can't** speak their language at break time.
11. Students **can / can't** ask the teacher questions.
12. Students **can / can't** make phone calls in class.

fight

shout

You can't be late

Writing

What are the rules in your college? Write sentences with **can / can't** etc.

e.g. In my college you can drink water in class but you can't eat.

1. Write about the rules in your college.

2. Cover the text and write this again.

Unit 6

What are you wearing?

Clothes

Vocabulary

1. Tick the correct word.

a.

☐ jacket
☑ jeans
☐ jumper

b.

☐ dress
☐ t-shirt
☐ shirt

c.

☐ shirt
☐ t-shirt
☐ jeans

d.

☐ jacket
☐ jeans
☐ jumper

e.

☐ suit
☐ shoes
☐ shirt

f.

☐ jacket
☐ suit
☐ dress

g.

☐ hat
☐ suit
☐ hijab

h.

☐ dress
☐ suit
☐ shirt

i.

☐ jumper
☐ jacket
☐ jeans

2. Match the words to the pictures.

gloves scarf socks skirt boots
trainers trousers sunglasses shorts

a.

____

b.

____

c.
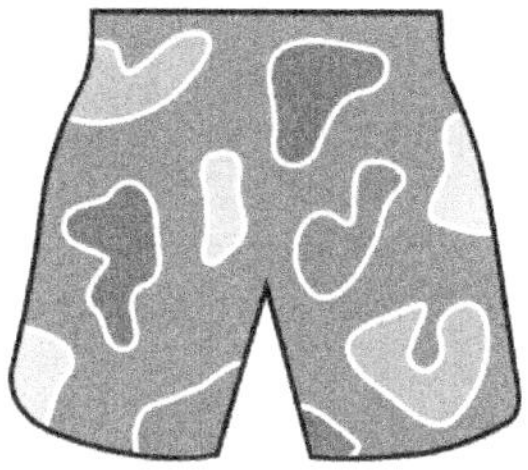
____

d.

____

e.
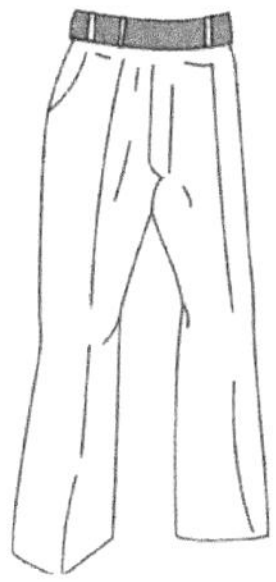
____

f.

____

g.

____

h.

____

i.
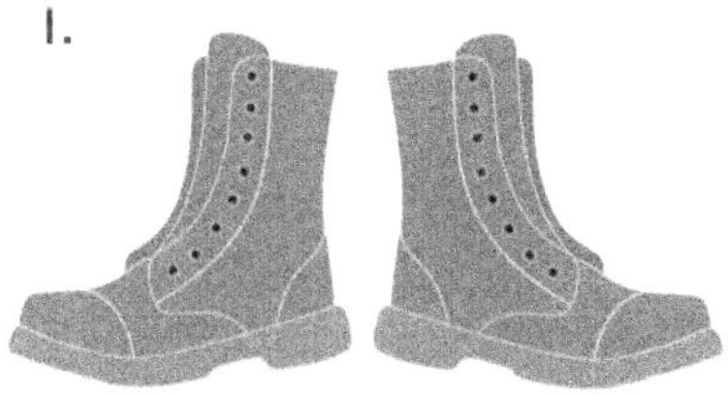
____

3. Fill in the gaps.

jacket shirt dress sunglasses shorts suit

~~jeans~~ shoes boots scarf trainers gloves

a. – What are you going to wear to the party?

– I'm just going to wear a red t-shirt and blue jeans.

b. It's so cold outside. Remember to wear a really warm ____________!

c. Many women wear a white ___________ at weddings in the UK.

d. It's my brother's wedding next week. He's going to wear a black _________, a white __________ and black ________.

e. It's really sunny today. Where are my ______________________?

f. My hands are so cold and I didn't bring my _____________ with me today.

g. I'm going to take clothes for the gym later. I need a t-shirt, _____________ and my ___________________.

h. It's very cold today. You should wear a jacket, hat, gloves and a __________ to keep your neck warm.

i. It's snowing and it's going to snow for a long time. It's better to wear __________ today and not shoes or trainers.

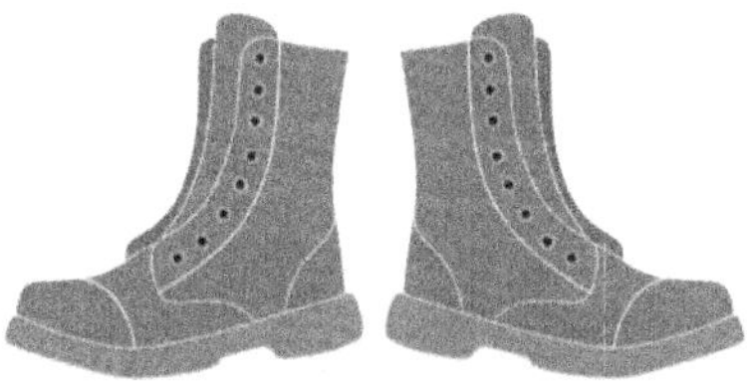

I love shopping for clothes!

Before reading

Look at the photo. Circle the clothes that you can see.

t-shirt jeans sunglasses
hoodie hat shirt scarf gloves

Reading

Read about Ali and answer the questions below.

My name is Ali. I love looking around the clothes shops in the city centre. I often go shopping with my friends and I love it when I find a nice new jacket or t-shirt. I shop online sometimes too but it's more fun to go to shops. In this photo I'm wearing a jacket, shirt and jeans. I'm wearing a hat and sunglasses because my friend took this photo in the summer.

1. Match phrases 1 – 5 with a – e.

1. I love looking	a. with my friends.
2. I often go shopping	b. this photo in the summer.
3. I shop online	c. I'm wearing a jacket and jeans.
4. In this photo	d. around clothes shops.
5. My friend took	e. sometimes.

2. True or false?

a. He's happy to go shopping for clothes. True

b. He always goes shopping alone.

c. He looks for clothes on websites sometimes.

d. He likes shopping online more than going to shops.

e. He's wearing shorts in the photo.

f. Ali's friend took the photo in the winter.

3. Answer the questions

a. What's his name?

His name is Ali.

b. Where does he like to go to buy clothes?

c. Who does he go shopping with?

d. What does he like more, going to the shops or shopping online?

e. What is he wearing in the photo?

f. When did his friend take the photo?

I love shopping for clothes!

Writing

Put the words in the correct order. Remember to use capital letters and full stops.

1. clothes shops   looking around   love   i

   I love looking around clothes shops.

2. online sometimes   shop   i

3. it's fun   the shops   to go to

4. city centre   i go   in the   shopping

5. my friends   i like   with   shopping

6. wearing   photo   and sunglasses in this   i'm   a hat

7. and jeans   a shirt   i'm wearing

Colours

Vocabulary and spelling

Write the answers to the questions in the crossword.

1. → The colour of the sky or the sea.
1. ↓ The colour of chocolate.
2. The colour of elephants or old people's hair sometimes.
3. The colour of sunglasses or coffee with no milk.
4. The colour of the sun or lemons.
5. The colour of rice or milk.
6. The colour of grass or broccoli.
7. The colour of pigs.
8. The colour of strawberries or tomatoes.

a pig

broccoli

lemons

I have a pink hat

Grammar: verbs, nouns and adjectives

1. Write the words in the table.

~~happy~~ ~~blue~~ ~~shoes~~ ~~scarf~~ ~~tall~~ ~~buy~~ ~~woman~~ ~~eat~~ ~~sleep~~ jeans
read pencil short do yellow gloves t-shirt blue rubber
bottle expensive walk listen student paper run sick like

Verbs	Adjectives	Nouns
sleep	happy	shoes
buy	blue	scarf
eat	tall	woman

2. Can you write more verbs, nouns and adjectives in the table?

Can you see the mistakes?

A. Grammar

The sentences below all have one mistake. Can you change them?

black jumper
1. She's wearing a ~~jumper black~~.
2. I wearing a blue shirt.
3. I'm blue jeans.
4. I'm wearing shoes brown.
5. I'm wearing a blue jeans today.
6. I'm wearing a white t-shirts.
7. I'm wearing blue jean.

B. Writing

What are you wearing today?

e.g. I'm wearing blue jeans. I'm wearing a black t-shirt and a blue jacket.

I'm wearing blue jeans

Vocabulary and spelling

The word 'jeans' has **ea** in it. Look below at more words with **ea.** Can you find the words and circle them?

~~meat~~ ~~jeans~~ beard tea year near read great head
break easy learn speak heavy sea early

s	i	h	e	a	v	y	e	s	c	g
g	j	h	g	r	e	a	t	s	m	r
o	c	k	l	e	a	r	n	s	e	a
r	j	e	a	n	s	b	h	m	a	y
e	m	t	a	r	y	t	e	b	t	e
a	l	h	b	e	a	r	d	r	v	a
d	o	e	e	a	y	a	t	e	a	r
n	e	a	r	u	s	p	e	a	k	o
b	e	d	e	a	r	l	y	k	h	w

I'm wearing blue jeans

Vocabulary and spelling

Put the letters in order to make a word. Every word has **ea**.

1. The man in the photo has a __beard__. (brade)
2. He's ______________ blue ________. (raweing / janes)

3. I can ____________ English and Arabic. (peaks)
4. I ___________ English in college. (nearl)
5. I _______ pasta, rice or _________ nearly every day. (tea / brade)
6. I _________ and write in college every day. (dare)
7. What time do you get up? Do you get up ___________ or late? (leary)
8. Do you live __________ college or far away? (rane)
9. My favourite __________ is chicken (mate)
10. We have a ___________ in college every day to go to the toilet or have a coffee. (krabe)
11. Do you think learning English is __________ or difficult? (saye)
12. He's 22 ___________ old. (yares)
13. Do you like _________ or coffee? (eta)
14. I like swimming in the _________ but it's too cold in the UK. (ase)

He has a beard

Vocabulary

Circle the correct word.

1. Colin

He's wearing **glasses / sunglasses** and a **suit / hat**. He has **short / long** hair. I like his **t-shirt / shirt**, tie and **suit / dress**. He is very smart in this photo.

2. Claire

She looks very **sad / happy**. She has **long / short** grey hair and she's drinking a cup of tea in this photo.

3. Angela

She's **smiling / crying** and looks so **happy / sad** in this photo! She has **short / long** hair and she's wearing **glasses / a hat**.

4. Mike

He has a **beautiful / sad** smile and grey hair. He has a **moustache / beard**.

5. Ali

Ali has a beard and he's wearing **glasses / a jacket** and a yellow **jumper / t-shirt**. He's **a young / an old** man.

I like your style!

Writing

Copy the sentences but add spaces. Don't forget to add capital letters and full stops.

1. coliniswearingglassesandasuit

Colin is wearing glasses and a suit.

2. hehasshorthair

3. clairelooksveryhappy

4. shehasshortgreyhair

5. angelalookssohappy

6. mikehasabeautifulsmile

7. alihasabeard

8. he'swearingayellowt-shirt

I'm wearing blue jeans

Writing

Write about yourself and a friend. What are you wearing? What colour is your hair?

e.g. My name is Faisal. I'm wearing black jeans and a white t-shirt today. I have short black hair. Ali is my friend. He's wearing blue jeans and a black jacket. He has long black hair.

1. Write about yourself and a friend here:

2. Cover the text above and write it again.

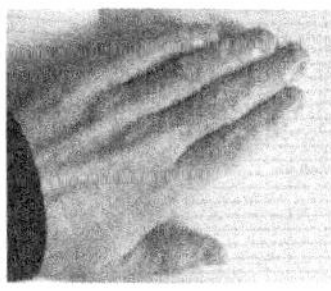

I'm wearing a red jacket

Writing

Copy the sentences but use contractions (e.g. I'm, he's, she's, you're).

1. I am wearing a red jacket.

   I'm wearing a red jacket.

2. She is wearing a red dress.

   She's wearing a red dress.

3. He is wearing a white shirt.

   ____

4. I do not have a hat today.

   ____

5. You are wearing a nice shirt.

   ____

6. We are writing about clothes.

   ____

7. I do not like wearing a hat.

   ____

8. He is wearing sunglasses.

   ____

9. She is smiling.

   ____

They're dancing

Spelling

1. Circle the correct spelling.

   a. They're **danceing / dancing** in this photo.
   b. He's **smoking / smokeing**.
   c. Do you **smoke / smok**?
   d. They are **writing / writeing**.
   e. We **write / writ** in our English class every day.
   f. Can you **dance / danc**?
   g. I'm **having / haveing** my dinner.
   h. Are you **using / useing** your phone? Can I **use / us** it?
   i. I'm **making / makeing** a cake.
   j. I **make / mak** a cake every Sunday.

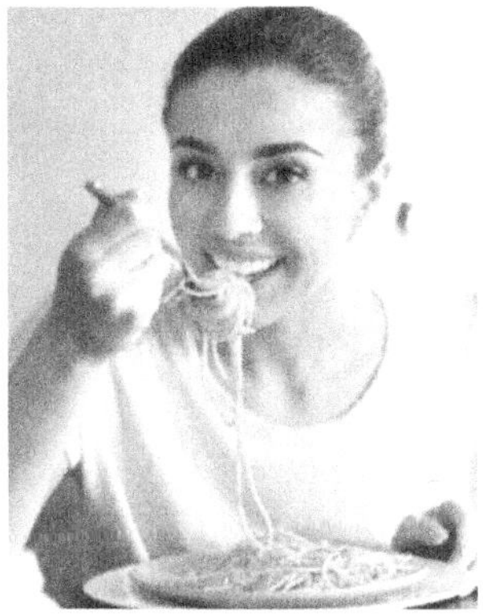

2. Fill in the gaps with **1 or 2** letters.
   a. I read and write at home every day.
   b. I like reading and writing.

   c. I ha___ coffee every morning.
   d. You can't smok__ in college.
   e. Are you us__ng that pencil? Can I us__ it?
   f. I like mak__ng cakes. I'm going to ma__ a cake tonight.
   g. Smok__ng is bad for you.
   h. Do you like danc__ng? I always danc__ at parties.
   i. Do you like reading and writ__ng? We wri__ in my class every day.
   j. What kind of phone do you ha___?
   k. I love this photo. My friend is smil__ng and looks so happy. She has a beautiful smi___.
   l. Can you call me back? I'm hav__ng my dinner just now.

They're dancing

Grammar: the present continuous

Finish the sentences. Use '**to be**' (am / is / are) and the verbs below. Don't forget '**ing**'.

clean play ~~argue~~ dance cook smoke

1. 

They are arguing.

2. 

She ______________________

3. 

She ______________________

4. 

He ______________________

5. 

They ______________________ basketball.

6. 

They ______________________

How much is that?

Numbers: money

1. Are these notes or coins? Write them in the table.

1p   £5   5p   10p   £20   50p   £1   2p   £10   20p

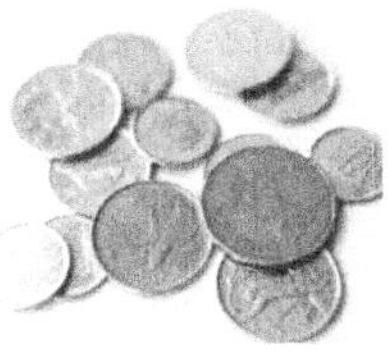

Coins		**Notes**	
1p	______	£1	______
______	______	______	______
______	______	______	______

2. If something costs £19.50 we usually say 'about £20.' Write these numbers again but use 'about.'

    a. 47p About 50p
    b. £19.95 ______
    c. £49.99 ______
    d. £78 ______
    e. 97p ______
    f. £9.95 ______
    g. £490 ______

3. How much is the total for these things. Use 'about.'

a. A red shirt for £2.99 and socks for £1.99. About £5

b. A black jacket for £44.99 and a hat for £5. ________

c. A jumper for £16.99 and a t-shirt for £7.99. ________

d. A hat for £12 and a t-shirt for £9. ________

e. Shoes for £35 and socks for £4.50. ________

f. A scarf for £7 and a shirt for £12. ________

g. Shoes for £35 and socks for £4.50. ________

h. Shoes for £14.99 and a dress for £9.95. ________

4. How much is the change? Use 'about.'

a. The shirt is £4.99 and you give £20. About £15

b. The jacket is £34.99 and you give two £20 notes. ________

c. The t-shirt is £4.75 and you give £10. ________

d. The jacket is £29.99 and you give two £20 notes. ________

e. The jumper is £14.99. You give two £10 notes. ________

f. The t-shirt is £24.99 and you give a £20 note and a £10 note. ________

g. The dress is £17.99 and you give a £20 note. ________

h. The hat is £2.99 and the socks are £1.99 and you give a £20 note. ________

i. The dress is £17.99 and you give a £20 note. ________

Unit 7

I love my phone

My phone

Vocabulary

Tick the correct word.

1.

☐ watch videos
☐ computer
☑ smartphone

2.

☐ gaming
☐ text
☐ call

3.

☐ text
☐ take a photo
☐ tablet

4.

☐ text
☐ take a photo
☐ tablet

5.

☐ laptop
☐ take a photo
☐ tablet

6.

☐ laptop
☐ gaming
☐ take a photo

7.

☐ gaming
☐ take a photo
☐ tablet

8.

☐ text
☐ computer
☐ call

9.

☐ computer
☐ watch videos
☐ laptop

I like my phone

Vocabulary and spelling

Find the words from the text about Hong in the Student's Book and circle them.

call ~~play~~ videos because games apps

funny phone texting watch friends

f	w	a	t	c	h	p	s	y	p
h	e	c	a	p	p	s	r	y	h
g	b	e	c	a	u	s	e	v	o
c	u	c	f	u	n	n	y	i	n
a	p	l	a	y	e	e	u	d	e
l	f	r	i	e	n	d	s	e	i
l	g	a	m	e	s	p	e	o	p
m	t	e	x	t	i	n	g	s	w

I like my phone

Spelling

Copy the text.

My name is Hong. I like my
phone. I have a smartphone, it is
an iPhone. My friend gave me
this phone. I like texting my
friends every day. I watch videos
on YouTube and TikTok. I like
these apps because the videos
are funny. I like videos but I don't
play games on my phone.

I need some information

Vocabulary and spelling

Find the words and circle them. Every word has **tion**.

~~information~~ ~~location~~ population celebration
nationality station connection

l	c	o	n	n	e	c	t	i	o	n
o	j	s	t	a	t	i	o	n	m	r
c	e	l	e	b	r	a	t	i	o	n
a	j	e	k	n	s	b	h	c	a	y
t	a	t	a	r	z	r	e	t	t	e
i	n	f	o	r	m	a	t	i	o	n
o	o	n	e	a	y	a	e	o	d	r
n	a	t	i	o	n	a	l	i	t	y
p	o	p	u	l	a	t	i	o	n	w

Come to college for registration

Vocabulary

Fill in the gaps.

population ~~connection~~ station registration
nationality location accommodation celebration

1. I can't use my phone here because there's no connection.
2. The ______________________ of the UK is about 70 million.
3. I went on holiday last week. The food was cheap but the ______________________ was expensive. We stayed in a great hotel.
4. We are going to London by train at 10 o'clock tomorrow so I want to get to the ____________________ at 9:30.
5. My best friend's wedding was a great ______________________. Everyone was so happy.
6. I'm from Iran but the most common ______________________ in my class is Syrian.
7. Do you know how to send a ______________________ on What's App? It's very good if you're meeting a friend and he or she is looking for you.
8. Please come to college for your ________________________ at 10:30 tomorrow. Bring your ID card and documents.

An e-mail to college

Writing

1. Copy but add spaces, capital letters and full stops.

   a. i'mverysorrybutican'tgotocollegetomorrow

   b. Ihaveanappointmentatthegp

   c. Icangoonfriday

2. Put the words in order.

   a. very sorry   go to   i'm   but i can't   college tomorrow

   b. an appointment   the gp   i have   at

   c. friday   i   go   on   can

An e-mail to college

Writing

Write e-mails to your teacher about appointments.

a. the GP   Monday

Hi Dave,

I am very sorry but I can't go to college on Monday. I have an appointment at the GP. I can go to college on Tuesday.

Thank you,

Fatima

b. the hospital   Wednesday

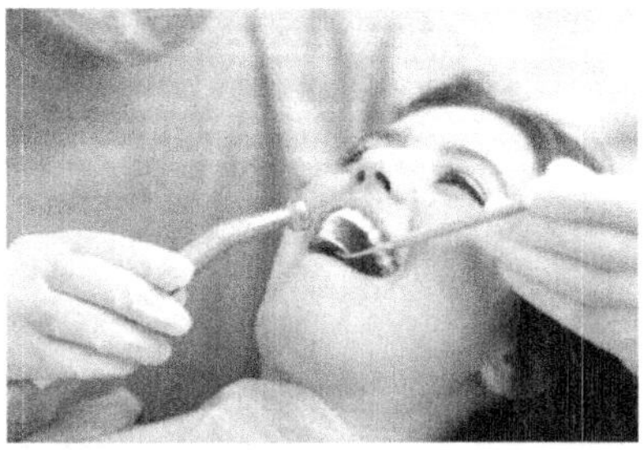

c. my solicitor tomorrow

d. the Job Centre Thursday

e. the dentist Monday

Do you like What's App?

Vocabulary and spelling

The word 'what's' has **wh** in it. Look at the words below with **wh.** Find the words and circle them.

~~what~~ ~~when~~ why where white who which

l	v	o	w	h	e	r	e	i	o	n
o	j	s	t	a	p	i	o	n	m	r
w	e	l	e	y	r	i	t	i	w	n
h	j	e	k	w	h	o	h	c	h	y
e	p	t	a	r	z	r	e	w	y	e
n	n	f	w	h	a	t	t	h	o	n
o	o	n	e	a	y	a	e	i	d	r
n	a	p	u	o	n	a	w	c	o	y
p	w	h	i	t	e	t	i	h	n	w

Where are you from?

A. Vocabulary and Spelling

Put the letters in order to make a word. Every word has **wh**.

1. Where are you from? (weerh)
2. I'm wearing a ______________ shirt and blue jeans today. (thewi)
3. __________ do you go to college? __________ days? (hewn / chwhi)
4. __________ time is your break usually? (thaw)
5. ________ do you live with? A friend? (owh)
6. ________ are you learning English? (ywh)
7. ____________ apps do you like? (chhiw)
8. ____________ do you live? (erwhe)
9. __________ do you usually have for breakfast? (awth)
10. ________ do you like college? (ywh)
11. ________ time do you usually go to bed? (awth)
12. ___________ are you wearing today? (awth)

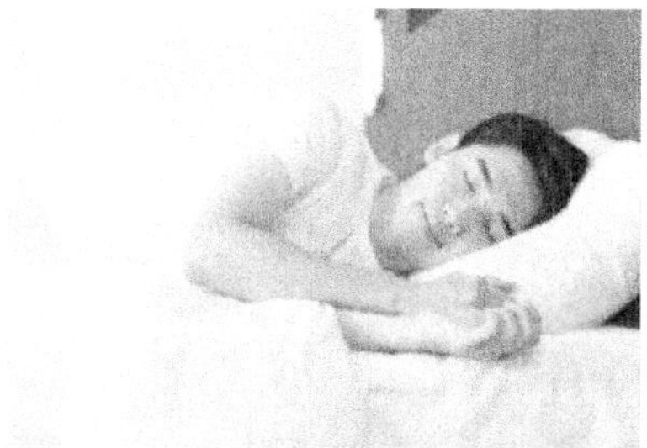

B. Writing

Answer the questions.

1. Why do you like college?

   I like college because I learn English and see my friends.

2. Where are you from?

   ____

3. Where do you live?

   ____

4. When do you go to college? Which days?

   ____

   ____

5. Why are you learning English?

   ____

   ____

6. What time is your break usually?

   ____

7. Which apps do you like?

   ____

8. What do you usually have for breakfast?

   ____

9. What time did you go to bed last night?

   ____

C. Speaking

Ask a friend some of the questions.

How r u?

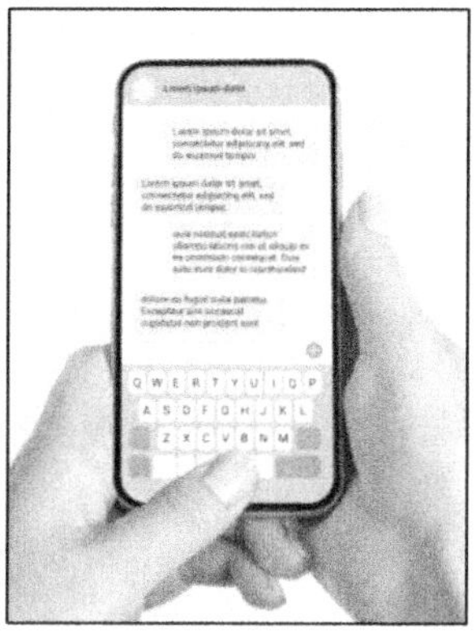

Writing

Write these sentences from texts but use complete words.

1. How r u?

   How are you?

2. R u free 2moro?

3. Do u want 2 meet later 2day?

4. It was gr8 2 c u last week.

5. R u ok? Y r u l8?

6. R u busy 2day? Can i c u 2night?

Which network are you on?

A. Numbers: phone plans

Read the plan and circle the correct word / phrase.

MAX7 Mobile

Mobile SIM only deal

50 GB
of 5G data

12-month contract
£15 per month

Unlimited texts
and minutes

18-month contract
Only £180

1. Name of phone network:	MAX7 Mobile / MIX9 MOBILE
2. Data:	15 GB / 50 GB / 200 GB
3. Texts per month:	18 / 50 / Unlimited
4. Calls per month:	200 / 2000 / Unlimited
5. 12-month contract price per month:	£12 / £15 / £18
6. 18-month contract price per month:	£10 / £12 / £18

B. Numbers: calculators

Use a calculator, if you need to, to answer these questions.

1. The 18-month contract is £180. How much is that per month?
2. Which is cheaper per month, the 12-month contract at £15 per month or the 18-month contract?

Your phone has a calculator. Can you use it? Watch a You tube video to learn about this or ask your teacher and classmates next time you are in class.

I love technology!

A. Reading

Read about Reza and answer the questions below.

My name is Reza. I love technology! I have a phone and a tablet. I have a Samsung phone and it's great! I love it! I got it from a shop in the city centre and I use it every day. I have a contract and it's not so expensive. I have lots of data and unlimited minutes for calls so I can phone my friends and chat for a long time. I have so many apps. I love You Tube, Snap Chat and I have some apps to learn English. I use Duo Lingo to practise my English. I love playing games on my phone and tablet too.

1. What technology does Reza talk about? Circle the words.

a phone   a tablet   a laptop   apps   You Tube
Tik Tok   Snap Chat   Duo Lingo   a PS4

2. True or false?

   a. Reza hates technology.
   b. He thinks his phone is excellent.
   c. His friend gave him his phone.
   d. His contract is very expensive.
   e. He can speak with friends on the phone for a long time.
   f. He has only one or two apps.
   g. He uses apps to study English.
   h. He never plays games on his phone.

B. Writing

1. Fill in the gaps below.

use lots learn love not chat games got

My name is Reza. I (a) ________ technology! I have a phone and a tablet. I have a Samsung phone and it's great! I love it! I (b) ______ it from a shop in the city centre and I use it every day. I have a contract and it's (c) ________ so expensive. I have (d) ________ of data and unlimited minutes for calls so I can phone my friends and (e) ________ for a long time. I have so many apps. I love You Tube, Snap Chat and I have some apps to (f) __________ English. I (g) ________ Duo Lingo to practise my English. I love playing (h) ___________ on my phone and tablet too.

2. Cover the text above and fill in the gaps.

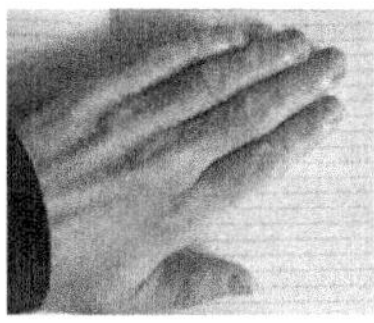

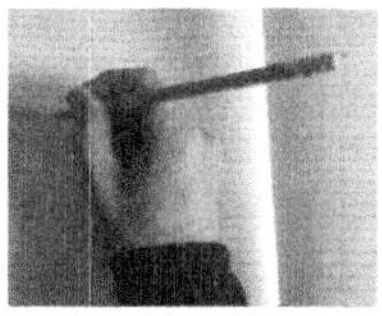

My na__e is Reza. I l__ve __echnology! I ha__e a ph__ne a__d a ta__let. I __ave a Samsung pho__e an__ i__'s grea__! I lo__e it! I go__ it fr__m a s__op in t__e __ity c__ntre and I us__ it ever__ d__y. I ha__e a co__tract and it's __ot so e__pensi__e. I ha__e lo__s of d__ta an__ unlimite__ m__nu__es f__r c__lls so I ca__ p__one my frie__ds an__ c__at fo__ a lo__g ti__e. I hav__ so ma__y a__ps. I lo__e You T__be, S__ap Cha__ and I h__ve s__me app__ to lear__ Engli__h. I u__e Duo __ingo to pra__tise my En__lish. I l__ve pl__ying ga__es on my pho__e and ta__let t__o.

I love my phone

Writing

Put the words in order. Add capital letters and full stops.

1. my phone love i

   I love my phone.

2. smartphone a have i

3. got i my phone a shop from

4. friends like texting my i

5. you tube watching I like videos

6. many apps so i have

7. games i like phone playing on my

8. some apps to learn i have english

I love my phone

Writing

Write about your phone. What do you do with it?

e.g. I have an iPhone. I text and call my friends and I have some apps. I watch videos on You Tube and I use What's App.

1. Now write about your phone.

2. Cover the text above and write it again.

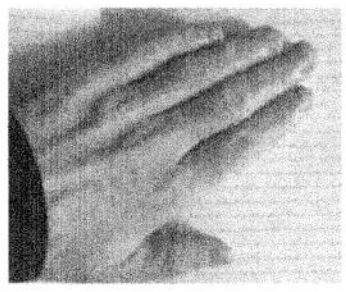

Phones and Computers

Vocabulary

Match the words to the pictures.

mouse charger keyboard controller

smartwatch SIM card console headphones speaker

1\.  ______________

2\. 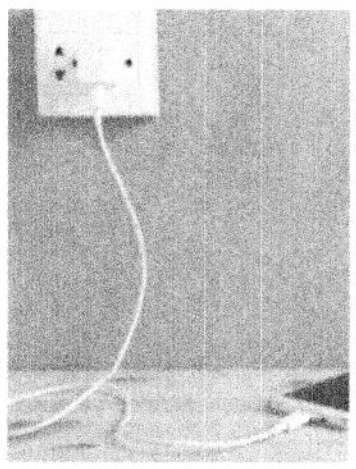 ______________

3\. 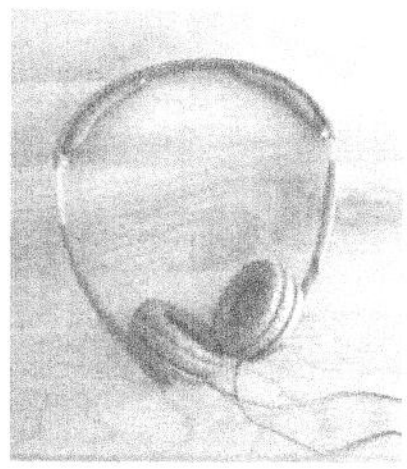 ______________

4\. 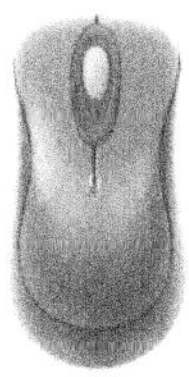 ______________

5\.  ______________

6\.  ______________

7\.  ______________

8 ______________

9\. ______________

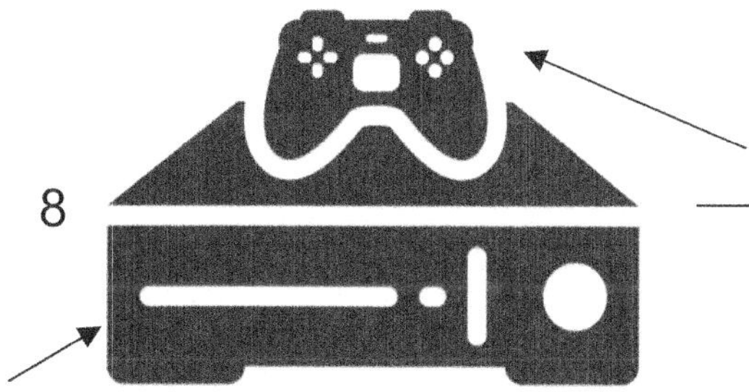

How do you use technology?

Vocabulary

Match the technology to the use.

smartphone ~~tablet~~ smartwatch mouse

speaker SIM card laptop console keyboard

1. I have apps on my phone but sometimes I like watching videos on a bigger screen so I use this. tablet
2. You can call or text your friends with this or play games. ____________
3. Use this to listen to music at a party. ____________
4. Do you like playing games? You connect this to the TV to play computer games with your friends. ____________
5. This is a computer that is easy to take to places like college or work. ____________
6. You connect this to a computer. It has all the letters and numbers so that you can write something. ____________
7. You can tell the time with this but it also has many apps! ____________
8. You put this in your phone. You can't use the phone very well if you don't have this! ____________
9. You connect this to a computer. It helps you click on words on the screen. It's also the name of a small animal! ____________

Unit 8

It's broken!

I've lost my phone!

Vocabulary and spelling

Write the answers to the questions in the crossword. Some answers go down!

1. Water is coming into my flat from the flat upstairs. There's a _____.
2. I have a problem because my phone isn't __________.
3. My TV isn't working. It's ____________.
4. I can hear my neighbours. They have a party sometimes or listen to loud music. They are very _____________! The opposite of quiet.
5. There are so many things on the floor. It's so _______ in here. Can we tidy up?
6. If something is broken you need to do this. Another word for 'fix.'
7. The thing that keeps a building warm in winter.

8.→ Where are my keys? Oh no! I've ________ my keys!

8.↓ People who don't want to work hard.

9. If you don't clean the kitchen then how is it? What's the opposite of clean?

You should bring a pencil to class

Grammar: should / shouldn't

Fill in the gaps with **should** or **shouldn't** and a verb from below.

should	speak (x2) ~~do~~ bring watch
shouldn't	go (x2) listen (x2) read (x2) ~~use~~

1. You should do your homework every day.
2. You shouldn't use your phone for so long late at night. It can be bad for your sleep.
3. Students ____________________ and write at home.
4. You ________________________ your language too much in class.
5. Students ____________________ a pencil and paper to class.
6. Students __________________ to the library sometimes. They have so many good books!
7. You _____________________ English outside class sometimes. Your speaking skills will improve more quickly.
8. You _________________ to bed very late. You will be tired the next day.
9. You _____________________ your notes from class after college.
10. You ________________________ to the teacher.
11. You _______________________ teachers on You Tube.
12. Students __________________________ to podcasts in English because they help you to improve your listening skills.

You should read your notes

Grammar: should / shouldn't

Look at the grammar below. Five of the sentences are correct but five have a grammar mistake. Which sentences are correct? Change the incorrect sentences.

1. You shouldn't go to bed very late. ✓

2. You should ~~doing~~ do your homework every day. ✗

3. You should listen to the teacher.

4. You should read your notes after college.

5. You should goes to the library sometimes.

6. Students should reading and writing after college.

7. Students shouldn't speak their language too much in class.

8. You shouldn'ot use your phone for so long late at night.

9. You should watch teachers on You Tube.

10. You should to speak English outside class sometimes.

You should do your homework

Writing

What should good students do? Write a sentence with **should** or **shouldn't**.

1. 

homework

You should do your homework.

2. 

forget your notebook

3. 

read your notes

4. 

practise writing at home

5. 

miss too many classes

6. 

bring a pencil to class

You should read and write at home

Writing

What **should** good students do? Use **should** and **shouldn't** when you write.

e.g. You should read and write at home. You shouldn't miss too many classes.

1. What should good students do?

2. Cover the text above and write this again.

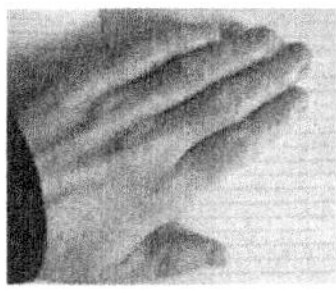

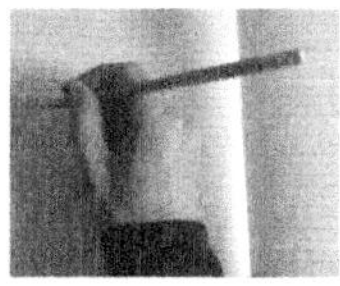

Oh no!

Reading

1. Look at the photos of Lisa and her phone. Then look at the sentences below and circle **three** which describe the phone.

It's a black phone. The screen is fine.

The screen is broken. There is a problem. There's no problem.

2. Read about Lisa's problem below and check your answers to exercise 1.

I really like my phone but I went shopping last week and something really bad happened. I was texting and walking at the same time. I wasn't looking and walked into a shop door! I dropped my phone on the ground! The screen is broken now and I'm so sad. I can use the phone. I can call and text my friends. I can use the apps too but it's very difficult to see anything. I went to a phone shop yesterday. The man in the shop looked at my phone and he says that he can repair it. I can get a new screen and it's not too expensive. I'm going to the shop tomorrow. I hope it will be OK because I really need my phone.

The shop door.

The screen is broken.

3. Put a – e in order. What happened first? Write numbers 1 – 5.

a. She walked into a door. ☐

b. Lisa went shopping. [1]

c. She went to a phone shop. ☐

d. She dropped the phone. ☐

e. She's waiting for the shop to repair the phone. ☐

4. True or false?

a. Lisa hates this phone. False

b. Lisa's friend dropped the phone.

c. There is a problem with the screen.

d. She can't use the phone.

e. The man in the phone shop has the phone now.

f. It's very expensive to repair the phone.

g. Lisa is going to the shop again in two weeks.

h. The phone is not important for her.

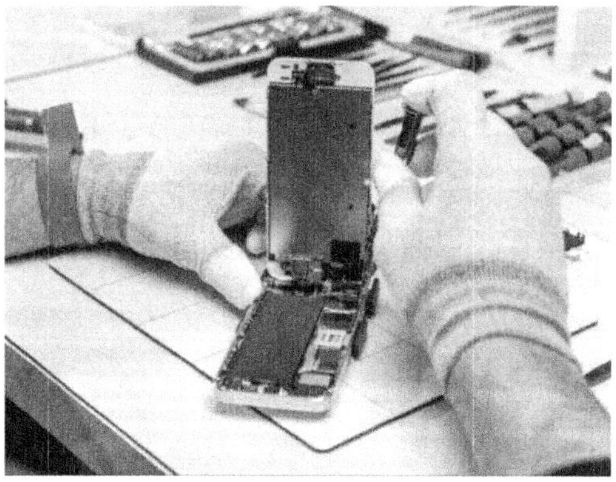

Oh no!

Writing

Put the words in order. Add capital letters and full stops.

1. happened really bad something

   Something really bad happened.

2. looking wasn't i

   ____

3. a shop door into i walked

   ____

3. on the ground my phone i dropped

   ____

4. use the phone i can

   ____

5. i went yesterday to a phone shop

   ____

6. a new screen get i can

   ____

7. it will i hope be ok

   ____

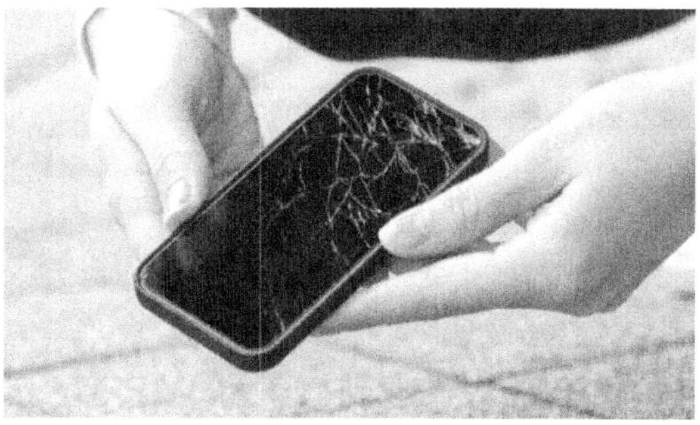

What can you repair?

Vocabulary and spelling

The word 'repair' has **ai** in it. There are some more words below with **ai.** Find the words and circle them.

~~hair~~ ~~train~~ paint air fair e-mail

chair repair stairs wait snail tail

w	p	a	i	n	t	b	h	s	e	u
r	i	r	w	p	o	t	a	u	m	p
e	y	r	f	e	r	r	m	a	a	w
p	c	w	a	l	w	a	t	a	i	l
a	h	a	i	r	t	i	w	i	l	n
i	w	i	r	t	s	n	a	i	l	a
r	s	t	a	i	r	s	i	r	w	i
s	g	a	i	c	h	a	i	r	q	r

I can repair my phone

Vocabulary and spelling

Put the letters in order to make a word. Every word has **ai.**

1. I'm going to repair my phone. (raprie)
2. I have short black ________. (hari)
3. I __________ my friend in Turkey every week. (e-lami)
4. I go to college by bus but my friend Mohammed goes by __________. (tarni)
5. There were three cakes and you had all of them! It's not ______! I want one. (rifa)

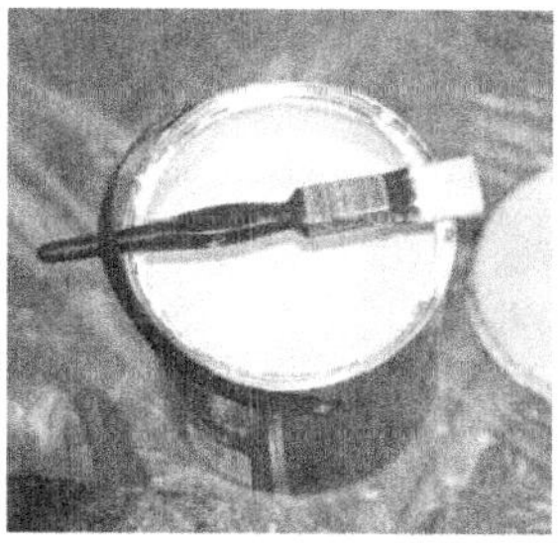

6. Can you help me _________ the living room? Which colour? Green? (pinta)
7. My friend is usually late. I often have to ________ for him! (wati)
8. Please sit down. Look, there's a _________ for you here. (chira)
9. I fell down and really hurt my leg. I was in a lot of _________ (pina).
10. It's very hot in here. Can you open the window to let some fresh _______ in? (ira)

How much is it?

Reading

Fatima went to a shop and got some things for her phone and computer. Look at the receipt and answer the questions.

1. What's the name of the shop?

   ____

2. When did she go there?

   ____

3. How many things did she buy?

   ____

4. How much did the mouse cost?

   ____

5. How much was it for everything?

   ____

6. How did she pay?

   ____

7. How much change did they give her?

   ____

TECH BASICS

62 Park Road

Bristol BS2 1OE

Tel: 0117 496 0999

10:17 on 19/03/2024

Keyboard	£12.99
Mouse	£8.99
Phone Charger	£7.99
TOTAL	**£29.97**
CASH	**£30**
Change	**£0.03**

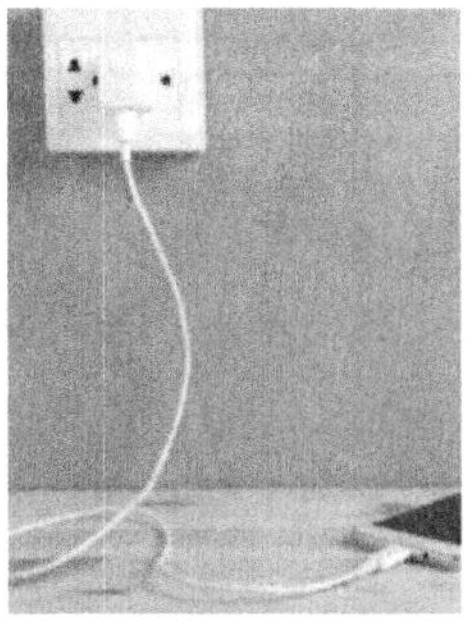

Prices

Prices

Fill in the gaps. In the example, the prices go up 5p every time.

a. 5p, 10p, 15p, 20p, 25p, 30p, 35p, 40p, 45p, 50p, ______

b. 1p, 2p, 4p, ______, 16p, 32p, ______, £1.28, ______, £5.12

c. £3, £6, ______, £12, £15, ______, £21, ______, £27, £30, ______

d. £10, £20, ______, £40, ______, £60, £70, ______, £90, ______

e. £1.11, £2.22, £3.33, ______, £5.55, £6.66, ______, £8.88, ______

f. £25, £50, ______, £100, £125, ______, £175, ______

g. £100, £200, ______, £400, ______, £600, £700, ______, ______

h. 1p, 4p, 8p, ______, 19p, 26p, ______, 43p, ______, 64p, ______

i. £12, ______, £36, £48, ______, £72, £84, ______, £108, ______

Unit 9

What's your job?

Jobs

Vocabulary

Match the jobs to descriptions a-l.

1. a police officer k
2. a farmer g
3. a barber ___
4. a security guard ___
5. a firefighter ___
6. a taxi driver ___
7. a shop assistant ___
8. a cleaner ___
9. a builder ___
10. a doctor ___
11. a nursery assistant ___
12. a teacher ___

a. He / she cuts your hair.
b. He / she cleans rooms in a place, e.g. a school/ college.
c. He / she helps you if your house is on fire.
d. He / she works in a hospital.
e. He / she drives you to a place.
f. He / she works in a shop.
g. He / she works with animals like chickens, cows and sheep.
h. He / she works in a school or college. Maybe you have one?
i. He / she works in a building and stops anything bad happening in that place, e.g. they stop people stealing from a building.
j. He / she cares for young children.
k. He / she helps stops people stealing your things or hurting people.
l. He / she works with a team of people who make new buildings.

Jenny

Reading

Read about Jenny and answer the questions below.

My name is Jenny and I'm a shop assistant. I work in a small shop in my local area. I like working in the shop. The customers and my workmates are all very friendly. I love chatting with the customers. We chat about anything. Sometimes we chat about the weather. Many people ask me, "How are you?" My manager is very nice too. I get a staff discount so everything in the shop is a little cheaper for me. I work part-time, from 10 o'clock to 2 o'clock, four days a week.

1. Read about Jenny and then circle the correct word / phrase below.

Name:	Jenny / Jane
Job	Manager / Shop assistant
Days	Monday to Thursday / Tuesday to Thursday
Hours	3 hours a day / 4 hours a day

2. True or false?
   a. Jenny works in a big shop. False
   b. The shop is close to her home.
   c. She likes her job.
   d. She only likes some of the staff.
   e. She never chats to anyone.
   f. She likes her manager.
   g. The customers pay more for everything than Jenny pays.
   h. She works all day.

20%

DISCOUNT

Jenny

Writing

Put the words in order. Add capital letters and full stops.

1. jenny name is her

Her name is Jenny.

2. works a shop she in

3. shop assistant a she's

4. likes she working the shop in

5. a small it's shop

6. likes she workmates her

7. part-time she works

8. four days works she a week

Jobs

Vocabulary and spelling

Write the answers to the questions in the crossword.

1. → Everyone who works in a place.
1. ↓ I work from 9 to 5. Every day I work an 8-hour __________.
2. People who work 7 hours a day have a ______________ job.
3. If you study in college you are a ____________.
4. What's your job if you teach in college?
5. The person who buys something in a shop.
6. In this job you cut hair.
7. People who work 2 or 3 hours a day have a ______________ job.
8. He/she works in a hospital.
9. He/she cleans rooms in a workplace.

Reza

Writing

Copy the text.

I go to college now but when my English is better I want to get a job. I don't know which job but I'm going to work hard in college so I can get a really good job. My friend has a job and now he has a car.

Which job do you want?

Spelling

Fill in the gaps.

Reza

I go to __ol__ege now b__t w__en my __nglish is better I __ant to __et a job. I d__n't kn__w w__ich jo__ bu__ I'__ goi__g to wo__k h__rd in c__lle__e so I __an g__t a re__ll__ goo__ j__b. My fri__nd h__s a __ob and __ow he __as a __ar.

Fatima

I __as a chef in __y __ountry and I l__ke c__oki__g. I w__nt to g__t a j__b in a re__taurant. I __an __ook f__od f__om __y country. I'm __tudying h__rd at __ollege j__st now. I w__nt to h__ve __ood __nglish __irst and __hen __et a __ob.

Asma

I am a s__udent n__w. In __y __ountry I w__rk__d in a sh__p. I w__nt to g__t a j__b in f__ture b__t I __on't k__ow __hich jo__. __aybe I ca__ w__rk in a __hop or an __ffice in fu__ur__. I ne__d to __ave __ood E__gli__h to h__lp me g__t a go__d j__b.

I’m a student

Writing

Copy and add spaces. Don’t forget your capital letters and full stops.

1. i’mastudent

    ____

2. iwasaabarberiniran

    ____

3. it’sagoodjob

    ____

4. themoneyisgood

    ____

5. iwanttobeataxidriver

    ____

6. maybeicanworkinashop

    ____

7. maybeicanbeachef

    ____

8. iwanttobuyacar

    ____

Which job do you want?

Writing

Write about jobs. Do you have a job? Which job do you want? Why?

e.g. I'm a student. I don't have a job. I want to be a taxi driver or a security guard in future. They are good jobs.

1. Write about yourself. What's your job? Which job do you want?

2. Cover the text above and write this again.

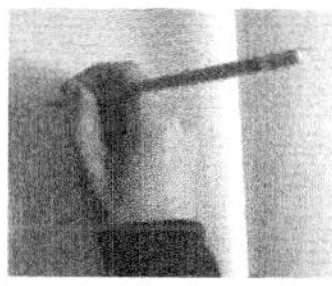

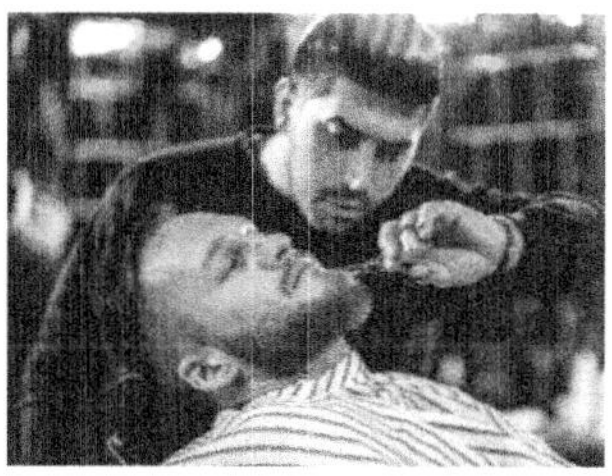

She's a teacher

Vocabulary and spelling

Many jobs finish with **er**, e.g. teacher, cleaner, driver. Find the **er** words and circle them. Some are jobs and there are some other words finishing with **er**.

~~teacher~~	~~barber~~	paper	water	river	plaster
computer	driver	cleaner	finger	tiger	ruler

t	c	o	m	p	u	t	e	r	h	f
u	b	f	i	n	g	e	r	r	o	p
t	a	b	r	i	v	e	r	e	m	l
i	r	u	c	d	r	i	v	e	r	a
g	b	t	e	a	c	h	e	r	w	s
e	e	c	l	e	a	n	e	r	o	t
r	r	w	r	u	l	e	r	e	r	e
p	a	p	e	r	w	a	t	e	r	r

He's a barber

Vocabulary and spelling

Write the answers to the questions in the crossword. Every word has **er**.

1. Use a pencil and ___________ to write notes in college.
2. → You can use this to write an e-mail.
2. ↓ He/she cleans rooms in a workplace.
3. Use this if you cut your finger.
4. Drink this if you're thirsty.
5. The _________ Nile in Africa is very famous.
6. He/she cuts hair.
7. Use this if you make a mistake when you are writing in college.
8. You have a thumb and four _____________ on each hand.

10

We had a great time!

A great day!

Writing

Copy the text.

I got up at 7:00 on Saturday.
Then I had a coffee and cleaned
my flat. After that I went to the
city centre with my friend. We
went to some shops and a cafe.
My friend had a cake and I had
a cup of tea. We had a good
time! Then we played football
before we went back home. In
the evening I ate pizza and ice
cream and watched TV. It was a
great day!

A great day!

A. Reading

1. Read about Asma. Why was yesterday a special day for her friend?

I got up at 7 o'clock yesterday. I had a shower and then I ate my breakfast. I went to college by bus after breakfast. The class was very good and I learned a lot. After college I met five friends because it was my best friend's birthday. We went to a restaurant and ate chicken and chips. It was delicious! Then the waiters and waitresses gave my friend a cake and everyone in the restaurant sang "Happy birthday to you!" We went to my flat in the evening and we watched a movie. It was a great day!

2. Put sentences a – f in order.

a. She had some breakfast. ☐
b. Asma got up at 7 o'clock. [1]
c. Asma and her friends sang "Happy birthday." ☐
d. Asma and her friends watched a movie. ☐
e. She went to a restaurant for chicken and chips. ☐
f. She went to college. ☐

3. True or false?

a. Asma walked to college.
b. She didn't like the class.
c. It was Asma's birthday.
d. They had chicken and rice.
e. Asma enjoyed the food in the restaurant.
f. The staff and customers all sang "Happy birthday."
g. Asma went to the cinema with her friends in the evening.

B. Grammar: the past simple

1. Find the past simple forms in the text on the last page and write them below.

a.	get up	______________	f.	learn	______________
b.	have	______________	g.	meet	______________
c.	eat	______________	h.	give	______________
d.	go	______________	i.	sing	______________
e.	is	______________	j.	watch	______________

2. Look at the verbs below. Circle the past simple verbs.

had go was watch learned sing eat meet
watched have sang learn give is ate went met

3. Fill in the gaps with the past simple of the verb in brackets.

I (a) ______________ (get up) at 7 o'clock yesterday. I (b) ______ (have) a shower and then I (c) ______ (eat) my breakfast. I (d) _________ (go) to college by bus. The class (e) ______ (be) very good and I (f) _______________ (learn) a lot. After college I (g) ______ (meet) five friends because it (h) ______ (be) my best friend's birthday. We (i) ________ (go) to a restaurant and (j) ______ (eat) chicken and chips. It (k) ______ (be) delicious! Then the waiters and waitresses (l) ________ (give) my friend a cake and everyone in the restaurant (m) _______ (sing) "Happy birthday to you!" We (n) ________ (go) to my flat in the evening and we (o) ___________ (watch) a movie. It (p) ______ (be) a great day!

A great day!

Writing

Put the sentences in order and add spaces, capital letters and full stops.

1. at 7 o'clock   i   yesterday   got up

I got up at 7 o'clock yesterday.

2. by bus   to   i went   college

3. very good   was   class   the

4. friend's   it was   my   birthday

5. we   and chips   ate   chicken

6. delicious   was   the food

7. sang "happy birthday"   in the   everyone   restaurant

8. went to   we   in the evening   my flat

9. watched   we   a movie

10. day   a great   it was

It was a great day!

Vocabulary and spelling

The words below are all **past simple verbs.** Find the words and circle them.

gave ~~was~~ learned had cleaned

played watched met lived went ate

p	a	t	e	u	g	a	v	e
b	i	l	c	w	a	s	n	c
l	w	e	n	t	f	x	d	l
i	l	e	a	r	n	e	d	e
v	p	l	a	y	e	d	u	a
e	l	w	n	u	r	m	s	n
d	w	a	t	c	h	e	d	e
s	h	a	d	n	c	t	n	d

It was a great day!

Vocabulary and spelling

Write the answers to the questions in the crossword. Some answers go down!

1. The past of play.
2. The past of live.
3. The past of give
4. The past of have.
5. The past of watch.
6. The past of clean.
7. The past of am / is.

8.→ The past of are.

8.↓ The past of go.

9. The past of eat.

A great day!

Writing

1. What did you do yesterday?

2. Cover the text above and write this again.

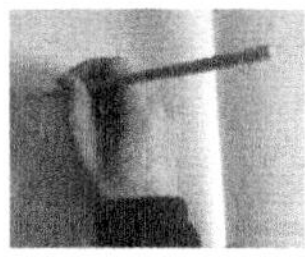

I really enjoyed myself!

Vocabulary and spelling

The word 'enjoy' has **oy** in it. The letters **oy** and **oi** often sound the same. Find the words and circle them.

~~enjoy~~ ~~join~~ boy coin noisy destroy

boil toilet oil annoy point voice

b	o	y	u	t	h	p	n	y
o	l	c	e	n	j	o	y	d
i	b	t	c	c	o	i	n	e
l	c	e	v	o	i	c	e	s
p	l	p	o	i	n	t	a	t
o	w	n	n	o	i	s	y	r
i	t	o	i	l	e	t	e	o
l	a	n	n	o	y	e	d	y

I really enjoyed myself!

Vocabulary and spelling

Fill in the gaps. Use the letters in brackets. You need to put the letters in order. Every word has **oi** or **oy**.

1. I really enjoy myself when I play football with my friends. (enyjo)
2. My friends has two kids, a ______ and a girl. (ybo)
3. We can have dinner after I ________ the rice. (lobi)
4. Excuse me, where is the __________ please? (loitte)
5. I'm going to ________ a gym next week. (noji)
6. I'm going to the shop to buy some ______ so I can fry some eggs for dinner. (lio)
7. My friend's kids have so many ________. (otys)
8. My neighbours are friendly but they are very __________. I can always hear music or TV from their flat. They really ________ me. (soiny / onnay)
9. Can you change £5? I want to buy a can of drink from this machine. I just need a £1 ________. (nico)

Camera story

A. Reading

Read the story about Dave's camera and answer the questions below.

Dave is a teacher. He went on holiday with his girlfriend ten years ago. They met two men, John and Bob, in a cafe. Dave gave John his camera because he wanted a photo. John moved back to take a photo, moved back more and then a little more. Then he ran! Dave ran but the man was very fast. Then Dave saw a police officer and shouted for help. The police officer ran and got the man. The police officer gave Dave his camera and he was very happy.

1. What's Dave's job?
   He's a teacher.
2. When did he go on holiday?
   ____
3. Who did he meet in a cafe?
   ____
4. Who did he give the camera to?
   ____
5. Why was it difficult for Dave to get the man?
   ____
6. What did the police officer do?
   ____
7. How did Dave feel at the end of the story?
   ____

B. Writing

Put the words in order. Add capital letters and full stops.

1. dave in went on holiday ten years ago

Dave went on holiday ten years ago.

2. met men he two in a cafe

____

3. gave his dave john camera

____

4. moved back a photo john to take

____

5. moved back he a little more

____

6. man was the very fast

____

7. got the police officer the man

____

8. the police officer his camera gave dave

____

9. happy was very he

____

C. Grammar: the past simple

1. Fill in the gaps with the past tense.

   a. Dave _went_____ on holiday ten years ago. (go)
   b. He __________ two men in a cafe. (meet)
   c. He ____________ with the men for a long time. (chat)
   d. Dave and the men ________ a really good time. (have)
   e. Dave ________ the man the camera. (give)
   f. The man _________ back to take a photo. (move)
   g. The man ________ very fast. (be)
   h. The police officer_______ the man. (get)
   i. The police officer ________ Dave the camera. (give)
   j. Dave ______ very happy. (be)

2. Write the story about Dave and his camera. Use the words below. Try not to copy.

   teacher holiday bar camera

   photo fast police officer happy

____

____

____

____

____

____

____

3. Cover the text in exercise 2 and write this again.

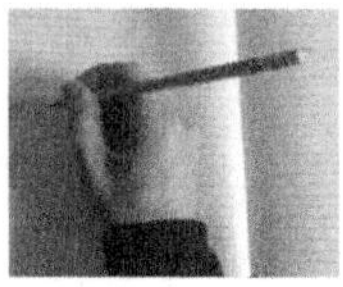

4. Do you have a good story from your life? Write it below.

Unit 11

The Summer

How was your trip?

Vocabulary

1. Tick the correct word.

a.

☐ the zoo
☑ the cinema
☐ the beach

b.

☐ trip
☐ the zoo
☐ a barbecue

c.

☐ the zoo
☐ the beach
☐ the cinema

d.

☐ a picnic
☐ a museum
☐ the zoo

e.

☐ the fair
☐ a barbecue
☐ a picnic

f.

☐ a museum
☐ the zoo
☐ the beach

g.

☐ the cinema
☐ a museum
☐ the fair

h.

☐ a picnic
☐ a barbecue
☐ the zoo

i.

☐ cleaning
☐ shopping
☐ camping

2. Circle the correct word.

a. I went to **the cinema / the zoo / a museum** last week and watched an amazing movie!
b. I love going to **the zoo / the beach / the cinema** with my friends. I love sunbathing and swimming in the sea.
c. I usually have a great time when I go **shopping / swimming / camping**. You can sleep in a beautiful place and it's cheaper than staying in a hotel.
d. I'm going to have **a picnic / a barbecue / dinner** with my friends in the park tomorrow. We are going to take sandwiches, fruit and chocolate.
e. I'm going to **a barbecue / a picnic / a restaurant** at the weekend in my friend's garden. We're going to cook burgers and chicken.
f. I love going to **the museum / the fair / the zoo**. I love seeing all the animals and taking lots of photos. My favourite animals are the lions and crocodiles.
g. There is a very good **zoo / museum / beach** in my city. You can learn so much and see so many interesting old things from all over the world.
h. I went to Blackpool last year. I went to the beach for a few hours every day and after that I went to **the museum / the zoo / the fair** to enjoy the games and rides, especially the roller coaster!
i. We went to Manchester for three days last year. It was a great **barbecue / trip / museum**!

The summer

Reading

Read about Reza and answer the questions in exercise 1.

My name is Reza and I'm a student. My college closes at the end of June for the summer holiday. I love college but I'm happy that I can have some free time in July and August. I'm going camping with three really good friends of mine. We're going to the Lake District. Do you know it? It's a beautiful place in the north of England. We're going to stay for a weekend in July. We're going to go for a long walk every day. We're going to be very tired in the evening! The Lake District is popular because everyone says it is really beautiful so I'm very happy about this trip. We're going to have a barbecue every night too! I just hope that we have some sunny weather as camping in the rain is not so nice! I'm going to take my jacket as it's in the UK so it might rain!

1. Circle the answers. Circle **one, two or three** words.

a. Name:	Amir Reza Rashid Riyad
b. The months his college is closed:	June July August September
c. Place he's going to visit:	London Lake District Peak District
d. What he's going to do there:	go camping have a barbecue go for long walks go to the beach

2. True or false?

   a. Reza is going to stay in a hotel.
   b. Four people are going camping.
   c. The Lake District is in the south of England.
   d. He's going to stay there for one week.
   e. He's going to relax all day.
   f. Many people visit this place.
   g. Rain is possible.

3. Fill in the gaps.

stay	sunny	because	place	might
every	happy	holiday	I'm	camping

My name is Reza and (a) _______ a student. My college closes at the end of June for the summer (b) ________________. I love college but I'm happy that I can have some free time in July and August. I'm going (c) ______________ with three really good friends of mine. We're going to the Lake District. Do you know it? It's a beautiful (d) __________ in the north of England. We're going to (e) ________ for a weekend in July. We're going to go for a long walk every day. We're going to be very tired in the evening! The Lake District is popular (f) _______________ everyone says it is really beautiful so I'm very (g) __________ about this trip. We're going to have a barbecue (h) ___________ night too! I just hope that we have some (i) __________ weather as camping in the rain is not so nice! I'm going to take my jacket as it's in the UK so it (j) ____________ rain!

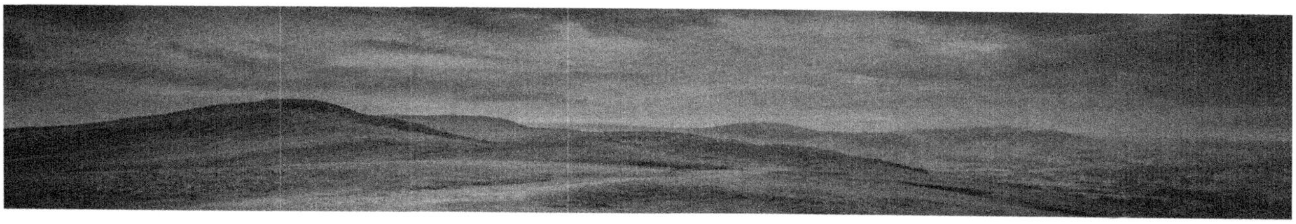

The summer

Writing

Put the words in order. Add capital letters and full stops.

1. have free time some that i can happy i'm

   I'm happy that I can have some free time.

2. to college i go from september to june

   ____

3. college summer holiday for the is closed

   ____

4. college i miss there is when a holiday

   ____

5. i'm my friends going to see

   ____

6. we have i hope that weather some sunny

   ____

7. and write i'm going every day to read books

   ____

8. on you tube to watch teachers i'm going

   ____

9. i learned in class i'm going to all the English study

   ____

   ____

I'm going to the gym

Vocabulary and spelling

The letter **g** has different sounds. The **g** in 'gym' sounds like the **j** in 'jacket.' The **g** in 'go' is different! Find the words with **g** or **j** below and circle them.

~~going~~ ~~jacket~~ age get juice job great Egypt

gaming January college July big orange

t	a	g	e	p	k	t	g	e	t	g
u	j	c	o	l	l	e	g	e	o	r
g	a	m	i	n	g	e	m	e	J	e
i	c	u	c	j	u	i	c	e	u	a
g	k	g	o	i	n	g	n	r	l	t
j	e	c	J	a	n	u	a	r	y	b
o	t	E	g	y	p	t	r	e	r	i
b	d	o	r	a	n	g	e	e	r	g

I'm going to London

Grammar: I go / I'm going

1. Choose the correct word. Remember that we use **I'm going** for **the future**.

   a. **I go** / **I'm going** to college 3 days a week.
   b. **I go** / **I'm going** to London in the holiday next month.
   c. **I go** / **I'm going** to the gym every day.
   d. **I go** / **I'm going** to see my friends tomorrow.
   e. **I go** / **I'm going** swimming this weekend.
   f. **I go** / **I'm going** to the cinema every weekend.
   g. **I go** / **I'm going** to Newcastle next month.
   h. **I go** / **I'm going** shopping every weekend.

2. Which sentences are correct? Which are wrong? Five sentences are OK. Change the incorrect sentences.

   a. I'm going to see my friends in the summer.
   b. I'm going play football tomorrow.
   c. I'm go to study English in the summer holiday.
   d. I'm going swimming at the weekend.
   e. I going to watch some movies in the summer holiday.
   f. I'm going to the gym tomorrow.
   g. I'm go to watch TV later.
   h. I'm going to cooking dinner tonight.
   i. I'm going to see my friends tomorrow.
   j. I'm going to cleaning my kitchen later.

I'm going to the gym

Writing

What are you going to do tomorrow? Use the word / phrase and write a sentence with '**going to**', '**not going to**' or '**might**.'

1. college

   I'm going to college tomorrow.

2. swimming

   I might go swimming tomorrow.

3. go to the cinema

   I'm not going to the cinema tomorrow.

4. gym

   ____

5. shopping

   ____

6. play football

   ____

6. do my homework

   ____

7. clean my flat

   ____

8. see my friends

   ____

9. watch a movie

   ____

I'm going shopping

Spelling

Look-cover-say-write-check

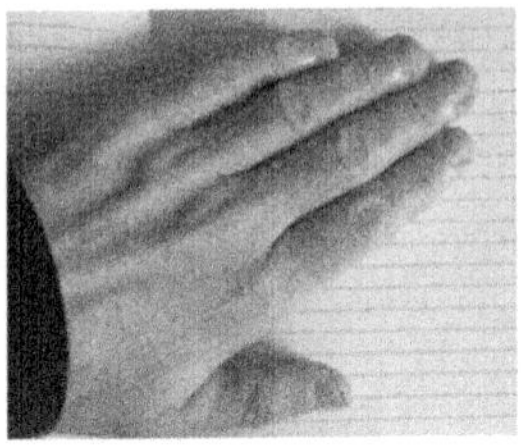

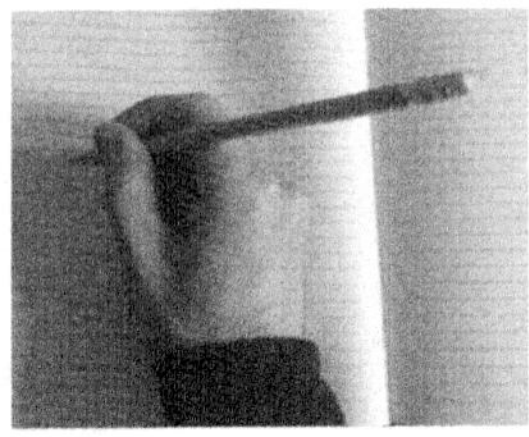

going	______	______	______	______
college	______	______	______	______
tomorrow	______	______	______	______
shopping	______	______	______	______
study	______	______	______	______
clean	______	______	______	______
summer	______	______	______	______
swimming	______	______	______	______
homework	______	______	______	______
weekend	______	______	______	______
might	______	______	______	______

I'm going shopping this weekend

Writing

1. What are you going to do **this weekend**?

2. What are you going to do **this summer**?

I'm going to the gym tonight

Vocabulary and spelling

The word 'tonight' has **ight** in it. Fill in the gaps below. Use the letters in brackets. You need to put the letters in order. Every word has **ight**.

1. I'm going to watch TV tonight. (nightto)
2. Can you check my homework please teacher? Are my answers __________ or wrong? (thirg)
3. You can't ___________ in college. You can lose your place. (thifg)
4. This t-shirt is too small. It's very _____________. (thigt)
5. I go to bed at _______________ every __________. (dimthing / thign)
6. It's so dark in here. Can you turn on the ___________ please? (thilg)
7. I'm going to the cinema ______________. (notight)
8. I __________ go to the gym tonight but I'm not sure. Maybe I will stay at home. (thimg)
9. I went to bed very late last ___________. (tingh)
10. I'm wearing a dark green shirt and __________ blue jeans today. (lihgt)
11. - Can I help you with your bag? Is it heavy?
    - Thank you but it's OK. It's very __________. (tlhgi)
12. I'm going to Paris by plane tomorrow. My _____________ is at ten o'clock. (tfhgil)

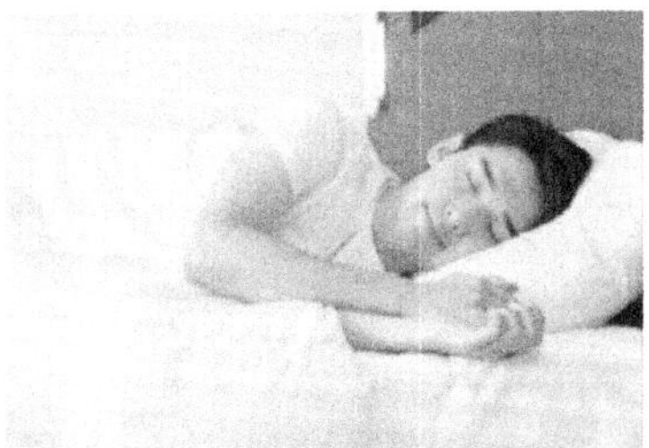

References

1. www.allkidsnetwork.com (free worksheets and worksheet generators fore teachers).
2. www.natcen.ac.uk (site giving figures regarding how people in the UK send their free time, used to compile the text about this in unit 2).
3. www.ethnicity-facts-figures.service.gov.uk (site with statistics regarding physical activity in the UK).
4. www.statistica.com (site with statistics regarding physical activity).

Printed in Dunstable, United Kingdom

79951156R00118